Libraries for the Future

Planning Buildings That Work

Papers from the
LAMA Library Buildings Preconference
June 27–28, 1991

Edited by
Ron G. Martin

Library Administration and Management Association
American Library Association
Chicago and London, 1992

Cover and text designed by Charles Bozett

Composed by Charles Bozett in Goudy and Avant Garde
on a Macintosh in QuarkXPress

Printed on 50-pound Finch Opaque, a pH-neutral stock, and
bound in 10-point C1S cover stock by Malloy Lithographing

The paper used in this publication meets the minimum requirements of American National Standard for Information Sciences—Permanence of Paper for Printed Library Materials,
ANSI Z39.48-1984. ∞

Library of Congress Cataloging-in-Publication Data

Libraries for the future : planning buildings that work : proceed-
    ings of the library buildings preconference, June 27 and 28,
    1991, Atlanta, Georgia / edited by Ron G. Martin ; spon-
    sored by the Library Administration and Management Divi-
    sion, Buildings and Equipment Section, Buildings for College
    and University Libraries Committee ; and co-sponsored by
    the Buildings and Equipment Section, Architecture for Pub-
    lic Libraries Committee.
        p. cm.
    Includes bibliographical references and index.
    ISBN 0-8389-0597-8
    1. Library architecture—Congresses. 2. Library build-
ings—Congresses. 3. Library planning—Congresses.
I. Martin, Ron G. II. Library Administration and Management Association. Buildings for College & University
Libraries Committee. III. Library Administration and Management Association. Buildings & Equipment Section.
Architecture for Public Libraries Committee.
Z679.L48 1992
727' .8—dc20   92-2252

Printed in the United States of America

96 95 94 93   5 4 3 2

Contents

Preface

Ron G. Martin

Editing a dozen papers presented at a two-day preconference and preparing them for publication were formidable tasks, but because of a good working relationship with the Buildings for College and University Libraries Committee, and the cooperation of the Buildings and Equipment Section (BES) of LAMA, and the presenters, my role as editor of these proceedings proved to be a most rewarding and satisfying experience.

When I attended my first meeting as a new member of the BES Buildings for College and University Libraries (BCUL) Committee, I volunteered to edit the proceedings of the LAMA BES two-day preconference on the future of library buildings. I did so with some trepidation, however, based on my earlier experiences as a member of the LAMA Publications Committee. Too often, it seemed, an editor attempted to pull together the papers of a preconference, conference, or program, after the event had occurred, only to experience inordinate delays in their timely publication, or he or she failed to consolidate the papers in publishable format for one reason or another. Understandably, after the papers were delivered, presenters would tend to go on to other ventures. However, my experience with this publication was quite the reverse—and I want to acknowledge those individuals who contributed to

the timely and well-organized process which has allowed this publication to be made available to the library profession.

First and foremost, the LAMA BES BCUL Committee's foresight in recognizing the importance of and need for a publication of the proceedings was critical. To ensure that a timely publication would follow the preconference, the committee requested that each presenter submit a print and computer disk copy of each paper, in publishable format, to me before the preconference. I initiated communication with the presenters months before the preconference, requesting information on the word processing software they planned to use and on the kinds of formats which would be required for the LAMA Office. By June 27, I had received paper copies and computer disks from all participants, and was able to follow the presentations and compare them to the written text, a kind of on-site editing. I would urge anyone who plans to edit a library program or conference to have the papers in hand, before conference time. So, thank you again to the members of the BES BCUL Committee for their foresight; it made my job much easier. A special appreciation goes to the chairperson of the preconference, Erla P. Heyns, for her outstanding leadership and organizational skills, for her advice and counsel throughout the publication of the proceedings, for writing the introduction, and for co-editing the bibliography which appears at the end of this book.

To each of the dozen or so presenters I extend my gratitude for meeting deadlines and for the outstanding relationship I experienced in working with them both before and after the preconference.

LAMA executive director Karen Muller, assistant executive director Barbara Uchtorff, and secretary Darlena Davis were instrumental in providing advice on the proper publication policies and procedures.

To ALA Publishing I express my gratitude for the workshop and orientation on the publishing process within ALA offered two years ago, and to Bonnie Smothers, ALA editor, who visited and informed the LAMA Publications Committee of procedures to follow when publishing with the Association. This knowledge has been most useful to my work in preparing these proceedings for publication.

Several individuals at Indiana State University deserve mention for their invaluable assistance:

Steve Hardin, reference/technical services librarian; Tom Robertson, library systems and automation research associate; Connie Richardson, office assistant; Joan Evans, administrative assistant; James Kinkade and Carol Walker, computing consultants, ISU Computer Center; ISU Libraries interlibrary loan services; and the ISU Audio Visual Center.

Also of vital importance to me was the granting of a six-month sabbatical leave by Indiana State University, which allowed me to concentrate fully on my editorial responsibilities. To the ISU administration, and to dean of library services Ronald G. Leach in particular, I express my appreciation.

Finally, I must express my heart-felt appreciation to my wife, Jennie, who graciously relented to transforming the living room of our home into my office for the six months. Thank you, Jen.

It is my sincere wish that these published proceedings will provide many libraries (public, academic, and other) with valuable information as they address future library building needs.

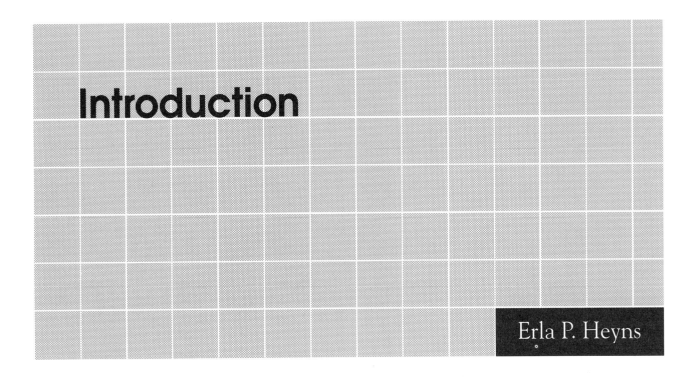

Introduction

Erla P. Heyns

As the chairperson of the program planning committee, it is my pleasure to write this introduction to the proceedings of the LAMA BES preconference "Libraries for the Future: Planning Buildings That Work," held June 27–28, 1991, in Atlanta, Georgia. The following planning committee members were invaluable to the success of the preconference: Donald Kelsey, director of library space and preservation planning, University of Minnesota; Tess Midkiff, director of library/media services, Shawnee State University; Carolyn Snyder, dean of library affairs, Southern Illinois University; and Anne Watts, coordinator, Downtown Branch, St. Louis Public Library.

A written justification for the preconference was presented to the LAMA Program Committee in order to secure support from LAMA. The following serves as a summary of that justification, as well as a summary of the preconference proceedings.

A preconference on this topic was deemed important because many libraries are currently in the process of planning new facilities and are in need of solid, practical guidance in designing libraries that will meet the future demands for library facilities and services throughout the country.

With that need in mind, the LAMA BES Buildings for College and University Libraries and the

LAMA BES Architecture for Public Libraries committees jointly proposed this two-day preconference. The preconference was designed to acquaint both public and academic librarians with new and existing space planning principles.

The BCUL Committee felt that the preconference was particularly timely, as evidenced in an article in *Library Journal* by Bette-Lee Fox (Dec. 1989, p.49) entitled "Ruins among the Splendor: Library Buildings 1989":

> One hundred eleven new public libraries were completed between July 1, 1988 and June 30, 1989, the greatest number since 1979. Over $347 million was used to fund 235 building projects (including 134 additions and renovations) in 44 states. Local funding was up 28 percent in 1989, accounting for 71 percent of total funding. But funding was up in all categories over 1988 figures . . . our Library Projects in Progress section . . . lists 949 new buildings in some stage of proposal or construction. That is an increase of 19 percent over the 796 buildings in progress in 1988. . . .

A two-day preconference format was selected because it provided attendees an opportunity to hear from experts with a broad base of experience in library buildings. The time period also allowed for personal interaction between conference attendees and speakers and networking among the attendees, which were also deemed valuable. In this setting, recent information, practical experience, and common concerns could be addressed in an effective and immediate manner.

The preconference was planned to address broader planning issues first, and these were reflected in the topics covered on the first day. The first three sessions were "Issues and Trends," "Outline of the Building Planning Process," and "Initial Roles of the Consultant and the Planning Team." Since the preconference was planned to address both public and academic library buildings, each session included two speakers, one representing public libraries and one representing academic libraries.

In order to provide an even broader perspective, reactor panels were used after two presentations, one on the first day and one on the second. The first panel was held after "Initial Roles of the Consultant and the Planning Team" session. The panelists were Donald Kelsey from the University of Minnesota and Sue Stroyan from the Illinois Valley Library System. Both are experienced consultants and were able to provide interesting insight and feedback on the presentation.

The first day concluded with a poster session of different libraries and institutions that provided a hands-on display of floor plans, building programs, and other documents associated with planning and building or renovating a library facility. Participants were:

Aaron Cohen and Associates, Croton-on-Hudson, New York

Anne Arundel County Public Library Headquarters, Millersville, Maryland

Arapahoe Library District, Littleton, Colorado

Arlington Central Library, Arlington, Virginia

Auburn University Veterinary Medical Library, Auburn, Alabama

James White Library, Berrien Springs, Michigan

Public Library of Charlotte and Mechlenburg County, Charlotte, North Carolina

Clayton County Headquarters Library, Jonesboro, Georgia

Crosby Library, Gonzaga University, Spokane, Washington

Indiana University-Purdue University at Indianapolis, University Library, Indianapolis, Indiana

Indiana University School of Medicine Library, Indianapolis, Indiana

Missouri State Library, Jefferson City, Missouri

New Haven Free Public Library, New Haven, Connecticut

University of Tennessee, Knoxville, Tennessee

The following libraries also displayed their program planning documents:

Hope College, Holland, Michigan

Lebanon Valley College, Annville, Pennsylvania

Arkansas State University, Jonesboro, Arkansas

La Salle University, Philadelphia, Pennsylvania

Willamette University, Salem, Oregon

Day two of the preconference concentrated on the planning process. The morning presentations centered on developing a program statement and included four speakers, three representing academic libraries and one representing a public library. In addition, a public library panel discussion followed. The three panelists, Anders Dahlgren, David Smith, and Lee Brawner, presented valuable insights into the planning process from their own perspectives.

The afternoon session centered on the issues of selecting an architect, through anticipation of construction. This session was highlighted by a "game" in which participants were asked to look at floor plans and identify specific problems associated with those floor plans. The purpose of this exercise was to make participants aware of the some of the problems associated with reading detailed building plans, and it set the stage for the discussion of the interpretation of the final working drawings.

The summary comments by Tess Midkiff and Anne Watts, based on personal experiences, drew the preconference to a rewarding conclusion. Midkiff's experience was with the construction of a new academic library facility, and Watts had the experience of working on the renovation of a Carnegie public library. They were able to pull together many of the comments from the speakers over the two-day period and make them relevant to what actually happens—"a perspective from the trenches" as they aptly put it.

The comprehensive bibliography at the end of these proceedings is a document based on bibliographies from many of the speakers and is intended to be a reference source for librarians involved in planning buildings.

Participants in the preconference included both public librarians (50+) and academic librarians (50+), representatives from other institutions, and architectural and consulting firms.

Several individuals deserve special mention for their help in making the preconference a success. The planning committee members, Donald Kelsey, Tess Midkiff, Carolyn Snyder, and Anne Watts, were invaluable in planning, organizing, and executing the preconference. I would also like to acknowledge the institutions with whom they are associated for their support through telephone calls, telefacsimile communications, secretarial support, postage, and release time to attend planning meetings.

The preconference could not have been a success without the help of the LAMA staff, including Karen Muller, Liz Miller, who started the project planning, and Barb Uchtorff, who took her place, and Darlena Davis. They provided support in planning the budget, preparing handouts, handling the registration, keeping the planning on schedule, and much more than I can begin to enumerate.

I want to thank the speakers for their excellent presentations. They met many deadlines and worked with us throughout the planning process to make sure that we had as little overlap in presentations as possible. I feel fortunate to have had the opportunity to work with such a talented and dedicated group of individuals.

I must also give honorable mention to Gloria Stockton, who chaired the BCUL Committee when I first accepted this assignment, and to Donald Kelsey, chairperson of BCUL during the planning of the preconference. I depended heavily on both of them for guidance and support in many areas. Kelsey's leadership and vast experience in LAMA made my life a lot easier.

Ron Martin, the editor of the preconference proceedings, worked with the presenters before and following the preconference to prepare their papers for publication. Because of his dedication and perseverance, the proceedings will be published in a timely fashion.

I would like to acknowledge Lynn Smith, planning and budget officer, Indiana University, Bloomington, for her work in preparing the initial budget for the preconference.

Last but not least I would like to thank the volunteers who helped with registration and other organizational matters during the preconference.

Trends and Issues

Joel Clemmer and David Smith

Overview

Academic Libraries

The biggest danger in library design is to assume that one responds to receptiveness by the college administration for a renovation or new library space project with a building program. The danger lies in missing the chance to reexamine the presumptions upon which the current collection and services are built, to design with the fresh perspective, to take advantage of the expertise and perspective in your own academic community as well as consultants, and to design a facility with the goal of meeting future needs rather than those of the past. The development of new information technologies is the most powerful among numerous important trends in academic librarianship. Much of what is discussed in this chapter relevant to academic libraries must deal with this set of problems, and it is a theme of many of the issues explored here.

A building project should begin with reexamination of the mission, goals, collection philosophy, needed staffing and service changes, and overall

management of the academic library. This process should precede actual building programming and take into account at least four areas of change. One is new information technologies and the extent to which they will affect traditional book and periodical collecting. Second, curricular trends and expressed student needs for study space must be assessed. Third, potential development of new ways to deliver library service to campus will affect design decisions. And last, planners must identify library staffing changes needed to accomplish all of the above. These issues will be explored in this chapter.

In his book *Academic Library Buildings*, published in 1973, Ralph Ellsworth recommended that facility planning presumptions be summarized "briefly and clearly" in a concept program, which also dealt with costing, space requirements, and other specifics. The concept program still is an excellent ideal but accomplishing it now is a much more complicated issue. College planners must first involve their communities in significant debate on topics such as those listed above. Essential to all these issues is the question of whether the academic library will survive at all as a physical space. Many think it will, but arguments for such a case are often perceived by administrations as self-serving. Librarians must clarify their thinking and be able to express the specific functions

Joel Clemmer is the director of the Macalester College Library in St. Paul, Minnesota.

David Smith is a consulting librarian from Hopkins, Minnesota.

of the academic library in the future to those outside the profession.

The preplanning process should also deal with typically recurring practical issues of academic library building. There are at least three. The first is money. In an unfortunate but understandable reaction to current funding problems, administrations often declare a cap on the number of dollars available, which means existing facilities must be renovated and expanded rather than new ones built. The trend toward renovation rather than new construction is documented in the annual *Library Journal* survey of building projects. Second, the latest money crunch causes colleges and universities to anticipate increased maintenance and operation expenses of both new and renovated buildings. The rule of thumb used by many college budget officers is to anticipate annual maintenance costs equal to 2 percent of the construction budget. These days, colleges often attempt to raise sufficient endowment through the fund-raising campaign for the new facility to produce that much annual income. Third is the issue of deciding who decides. Given the professed but erratically exercised tradition of collective decision making in academia, the earlier this issue of authority is cleared up, the better. In the academic community, a strong library director can be very influential in decisions regarding service and collection layout, user facilities, and staff station designs. Because the library has a strong symbolic meaning to the academic community, however, exterior appearance, interior ambience (including artwork), and, to a certain degree, location tend to be communal in nature and therefore lend themselves to a more distributed decision-making process.

Finally, planners must deal with the recurring issue of including other departments in a new or renovated library. Between attempts by administrators to kill multiple birds with one building stone and the desire of many academic departments for unhindered hands-on access to library resources and space, this decision can be a battle for the academic librarian. Influenced by functional relationships, librarians would rather be discussing the potential place of academic computing or media services in the facility, rather than the English department or whichever is the refugee department of the moment. If the librarian is able to communicate the need for security of the facility and for one uncompromised point of control (generally the exit gate), the administration often

will be sympathetic to resistance to such imperialism. There has not been a strong trend toward the inclusion of academic computing facilities in new libraries, except perhaps for a microcomputer laboratory often administered by computing services. Academic library cooperation with computing departments seems more often to be expressed in strategic planning, assistance in implementing systems, and sometimes administrative relationships.

Serious consideration often is given to inclusion of media or audiovisual services in the new academic library. Librarians have been preaching to each other about information in a multiplicity of formats, and here is a clear test case of how serious they are. Should the student who is curious about Hamlet have the opportunity to choose between the print and video versions under one roof, or even on the same shelf? Given the recent explosive growth of prerecorded video, it is surprising that many library building plans do not at least seriously consider including media collections. Admittedly, the practical consequences can be very great even in the small college environment. Minimal production facilities, for example, could require more than 5,000 net square feet. Many institutions explore possible separation of software collections, such as videotapes, and design library space for them as a compromise.

In conclusion, the prospect of designing and building new or renovated library space means that the librarian must engage his or her community in discussion of a number of both long-term and immediate planning issues. These issues will be explored in more detail later in this chapter.   J. CLEMMER

Public Libraries

Andrew Carnegie is dead. Long live Andrew Carnegie. Public librarians frequently comment in their discussions of building needs about the negative aspects of the abundant Carnegie buildings. Many librarians, however, have come to appreciate the impact of Andrew Carnegie on public libraries and what represents the development of a type of library unlike any in the world. The current dilemma is one of responding to success. With growing momentum through this century, public libraries have generated increasingly greater numbers of users. The new formats in technology have provided libraries with unlimited opportunities to offer unique and substantial services in the communities that they serve. The problem being encountered in many libraries, Carnegie building or not, is that the public libraries' success has outgrown the space available for collections, services, users, and staff. In the United States greater and greater sums of money are being spent each year on public library construction. Andrew Carnegie's gift back at the turn of the century amounted to some $57 million, which went into the construction of some 1,800 libraries in the United States alone.

More recent statistics, prepared by *Library Journal*, show that during 1989, expenditures for recorded public library construction in this country of over two hundred new libraries, renovations, and additions amounted to almost $350 million. Many libraries involved in building programs have not submitted any information to the recording sources. Public library construction and, therefore, public library planning are escalating at an astounding rate. In many communities, libraries that were built just fifteen or twenty years ago are no longer adequate and are either being replaced entirely or adding substantial additions.

There are a number of planning factors that have influenced consolidation of current trends in public library buildings. One is the cooperation between libraries. Libraries have been combined in federations and systems. They have been organized by county and district. A great cooperative attitude has developed among public libraries, allowing open access, in some cases on a statewide basis, and this in turn has increased both the use of and the pressure on libraries.

Space utilization is another important planning factor. How much space can be gained by pushing tables and chairs around? The simple truth is that library space is already so compressed that something must be removed in order to gain any space.

Another factor, particularly at this time when the public library's operating and capital funds are in short supply, as are the funds for other institutions such as schools, is the pressure to combine public schools and public library facilities.

The image of the "popular merchandised library" that has been generated through some of the Public Library Association (PLA) planning and role-setting processes in recent years and an opposing attitude that the library still remains the "people's university" create a dichotomy of possible models for the types of collections and services that libraries should be providing. Because of this popular-

ization, some libraries are turning away from the traditional stack and reading room organization to one that incorporates a higher level of merchandising in an attempt to attract use more as a bookstore or video store might. Certainly in the location of the facilities is an attempt to compete for the potential library user in the general recreational, leisure time, and intellectual marketplace.

Significant factors that are becoming more and more pressing in libraries are the organization of space and access to buildings and collections, in terms of making them fully accessible to persons with some form of disability as well as to a population that is growing older and, simply because of decreased visual acuity and physical flexibility, needs different types of collection layouts and shelving heights and better signage.

A very serious problem is the need to operate bigger, better, more sophisticated libraries with a diminishing staff budget that requires libraries to be as efficient as possible, and do more with less. This trend is just beginning and will become more and more serious during the next few years. There is, in fact, across the country a great deal of concern on the part of users of libraries as well as the general tax-paying public that libraries have exceeded rational boundaries of taxing limits. This perception is going to have a serious impact on all public libraries if not directly on academic libraries. There is a wide variety of elements at work now. The traditional libraries of the past are, for the most part, inadequate to meet new and present library uses and needs. Public libraries have achieved unprecedented success in terms of the increasing number of users that are coming into them every day. Occurring simultaneously with this great success are the withering of financial support and the increasingly intense competition for financial support that will allow public libraries to do as good or better jobs. The question then is how can public library buildings be planned for the future to take into account the needs that have been established and to recognize new technologies at a realistic, achievable cost. This chapter will discuss some of the commonalities as well as some of the differences in planning public and academic library buildings. A major purpose of this chapter is to increase awareness of issues, both general and specific, upon which can be hung many specific and detailed points contributed by the authors of subsequent chapters. D. SMITH

Space Needs

Academic Libraries

From the academic librarian's perspective, it is entirely correct that a new emphasis is required on the assessment of needs preceding precise planning of a new or renovated library facility. In academia, this trend often is expressed by questioning the basic future of the library on campus in the face of alternative ways of retrieving scholarly information. For example, if one agrees with F. W. Lancaster that the printed book is doomed, then to what extent does one need to apply the Association of College and Research Libraries (ACRL) standards on collection space? Second, if students and faculty retrieve needed information over an electronic campus network, should public service spaces be included in the physical library? Many campus administrators ask these questions before approving a library project. A strong recommendation is to provide at least a year for strategic library planning, so as to bring together people concerned about these issues and to coordinate the approach the campus wants to take to them. This preplanning period can be a very effective way to raise campus consciousness of library issues.

There are at least four primary roles for an academic library on campuses of the future that have strong architectural implications. Students will still need a well-designed facility for study and prefer that the space be shared by other readers, even though they also want a secure individual space for themselves. Other spaces on campus, such as classrooms and dorm rooms, usually are not adequate. No one has surpassed sociologist Robert Sommer's work in the 1960s in analyzing the preferred study environment.[1] Second, face-to-face consultation with information professionals will be increasingly important as students require navigational guidance through the multilevel world of digitalized information resources. As the business and professional worlds have found, electronic communication is not yet a perfect substitute for face-to-face consultation. The house in which such consultation occurs can be called a *library*. Third, libraries will participate in the continuous generation of innovative service based on new information technologies that will not necessarily begin their lives cheaply enough or robustly enough to be distributed to people at their workstations on campus. There probably will be a continuing stream of new technologies housed in the library that clients will come in to use, even while the expectation is that access eventually will be distributed. Finally, print publication is not going away. The number of titles published annually in the United States is decreasing but still stands at over 45,000 per year. We still need to build shelving and we still need a house for the physical collection. The academic library facility will continue to be the sum of spaces for public access and use, for staff, and for collections.

J. CLEMMER

Public Libraries

The assessment of library space needs is, or has been in the past, a preliminary step in library building programming. This needs assessment has grown in importance over the years as libraries have found that assessment of need is not merely an expediential enlargement of their present collection projections but, rather, involves a whole variety of factors. It involves the needs of the users and their expectations of the library over, in some cases, a fairly substantial time. It involves the needs of the staff members, how they will work within the library, what tools they need to adequately serve the public. One of the most important needs centers around the type of collection the library is going to house. This issue has become much more complicated, regardless of the institution, because of the various nonprint and electronic formats that the library has added to its traditionally print collections. The assessment of needs program has thus become much more important and much more expansive in determining what library buildings should include, not only in terms of capacities but also in terms of the features and facilities of the building, which will respond to the needs of the general supporting population. In the case of the public library, taxpayers are going to be involved in operating and maintaining the building over a long time, so the assessment of library space becomes not just one of simple measurement but an examination of the library's programs of service. This examination should include the opportunities toward which the library intends to move over the next ten to fifteen years, and the resources that go into developing new services and new programs that the library may be just beginning to anticipate.

D. SMITH

---

1. Robert Sommer, "Reading Areas in College Libraries," *Library Quarterly* 38 (July 1968): 249–60.

Needs Assessment

Public Libraries

One thing that frequently occurs in planning schedules, particularly when such planning is done by professionals other than librarians, is that the building needs assessment is allocated three to four weeks before the serious business of programming starts and then on to the design of the building. Three to four weeks to assess the needs of any library of size is totally inadequate because frequently the library has changed very little physically or operationally for years. Frequently a building is a catalyst that encourages libraries to plan when they have not planned in the past, depending instead from year to year on the gentle guidance of public need and questioning inquiry for different materials, and basically the budget of the library. So the time involved to do an adequate needs assessment should not be understated.

As to the participants, it is very important to involve users, it is very important to involve the staff, and, if at all possible, to involve those persons who ultimately will have to make the financial commitment to build the library specified in the assessment. So, a number of techniques and adequate time should be considered in the needs assessment, which in many cases is a more detailed and involved process than the actual programming of the building. Once the present foundation is known, along with current service programs and what those should be in the future, the programming part falls into place quite rapidly.

The PLA process for planning and role setting for public libraries is an excellent tool to use. To reiterate, you must know:

1. Current capacity
    Resources
        Collection: size by format, rates of circulation
        Staff: service points and staff
        Building: allocation of existing space
    Performance
        Users: who uses and will use the library
        Type of use: how is library used, how will it be used
        Level of use: circulation rates, visits to library, information contacts, turnover
    Environment
        Population: projected growth
        Economic: ability to pay for capital and operating costs
        Political: attitudes toward spending and the library
2. Where should the library be ten to twenty years from now?
    Goals and objectives
        Services: retention of existing and development of new
        Resources: staff, funding, collection
        Management: organization of staff and library operation
3. What is needed to achieve these goals and objectives? Remember, the library building is a means, not an end, in the provision of high-quality public library service.

Unfortunately, public librarians, library trustees, and architects have leaned on the crutch of American Library Association (ALA) standards and guidelines promulgated in the 1960s, and sometimes having their antecedents in the 1930s, 1940s, and 1950s. As a result, in planning the initial allocation of space needed in a library building, planners have looked on the chart and determined that for a particular population size, 0.5 or 0.7 square feet per capita are needed. Through simple multiplication they then come up with an ideal building size, which generally has a diminishing basis in reality. But it is a comfort that planners have taken something with an ALA imprimatur. Such formula planning takes little account of future needs. It is apparent in public libraries as well as in academic libraries that much of the seating that now appears in public library building programs is for special purposes, so the question that needs to be addressed by planners is does one give up 20 percent or 30 percent of the general seating to accomplish this, or does one now add to that amount? A far better way to develop a plan for building allocations of space, apart from standards and guidelines, is to become substantially involved in how much space it takes to provide adequate shelving for certain sizes of collections, and how much space it takes to provide for the specific amount of seating needed. One can then build, by a block-by-block-of-space approach, the amount of square footage that is going to be needed in a specific part of the building and put it all together into a consolidated assessment of space needs, which may have little relationship to per capita calculations. It's interesting to see that the typical

Carnegie library, built at the turn of the century with perhaps 2 square feet per capita, is now being replaced by a high-tech public library where planners are proposing to put 0.6 of a square foot of space per capita into a library that will incorporate features and services never dreamed of when the original building went up.

The LAMA Buildings and Equipment Section's Library Standards for Physical Space Requirements Ad Hoc Committee is currently studying specific, realistic space requirements for all special and general elements of a library building. These space guidelines, it is hoped, will be issued by ALA in the not-too-distant future and, at least for a time, will provide far more accurate and useful information as to what goes into the makeup of space for public and academic libraries.   D. SMITH

Academic Libraries

Not surprisingly, putting together planning teams in academic libraries is messy, time consuming, and politically sensitive. It is useful to think in terms of a two-tiered committee planning structure with appropriate ties between the committees. The more librarianly sorts of questions about service layout and housing of collections ought to be planned by a committee dominated by the library itself, often supplemented by a pre-existing library advisory committee representative of students and faculty. The board of trustees, the higher-level administration, and others will care greatly about overall budget and what the building as a whole says to campus, and these groups deserve a committee context in which to express their concerns. Add all this together and you get an underlining of the point made earlier about providing enough time for communication and needs assessment.

As the planning committees that have vicariously been put together begin working on a proposed library project, it is well to make them aware of the standards that have developed in the library field for the design of facilities and to encourage discussion of these standards. In the course of doing so, it is also very well to work with these standards not as literal rules to be followed without any sort of evaluation but as guidelines in an attempt to assess how standards fit into your particular context, be it a campus or a public library situation. The most common areas of confusion on the academic side include the effect of a heavy commuter population, typically found in community colleges and increasingly in four-year institutions as well. It's often assumed that a large number of commuters in the population will decrease the need for seating in the library. That needs to be discussed. Some colleges will point out that their commuters like to study on campus because of the lack of adequate facilities at home. That is an institution-by-institution sort of decision. Second, when reviewing standards, such as those published by ACRL, one must give very special consideration to special services, such as separate bibliographic rooms, media facilities, and after-hours study areas. These usually demand adding square feet to the net result of standards. Third, campus planners should consider very carefully adequate space for staff in the facility. The development of new information technologies, especially in public services, has not halted the need for staff growth but added to it. At the same time, additional space must be added to staff workstations for equipment. Finally, be very careful about the definition of the seating in the library. Are free-access, open, general study seats being counted or are those seats that are dedicated to special functions being counted? There tends to be an increasing proportion of special-function seats in academic libraries and planners should ensure that an adequate proportion of the full-time equivalent (FTE) student body still can be accommodated in open, general study seats.

J. CLEMMER

Expansion Potential
Academic Libraries

In the academic context, the issue of expansion of the library building in the future is very much commingled with the flexibility built into the new library building. The physical expansion of academic libraries that has occurred over the past two or three decades may not continue in the future. This possible reduction means that more librarians will be faced with the issue of living within the same four walls for a longer period than was previously the case. The issue of architectural flexibility must, therefore, be very carefully examined. There are two stumbling blocks in this area. One is the fact that true electrical flexibility, now so critical to functional flexibility, has yet to be achieved. Wire management internal to furnishings has come a long way, but point of connection to building systems continues to be a form of electrical boat anchor. Walker ducts, power poles, flat cable—all have either practical or aesthetic detriments. Second, the current architectural climate of post-modernism seems very concerned with definition of individual spaces within the building and with decorative architecture elements. These are expressed by non-uniform lighting, the use of interior walls to break up space, decorative columns and pediments, and so forth. Library planners should understand and be careful with this trend. Such designs increase user satisfaction with the space, but frankly do not offer the functional flexibility of the wide-open, undifferentiated spaces of the modernist libraries designed in the 1960s and early 1970s.[2] Finally, there is a critical precondition to planning library expansion and that is the need for agreement on issues of centralization versus decentralization of resources. In the academic context, this issue is often expressed in terms of branch libraries and intracampus networking. That is, with the development of online resources available to campus, are the large centralized libraries of the past still needed? In addition, many academic departments still want to develop their own branch libraries and decentralize traditional collections.

There is not much persuasive evidence in the academic environment that the development of new access points to information will decrease traffic to a centralized facility. Until electronic networks fill all the needs served by a library facility, both intellectual and sociological, it is probably more accurate to consider networking as a supplement to rather than a substitute for a central physical library. Networking is a solitary kind of activity that does not fulfill the perceived needs of many students who desire a place with other people engaged in the same activity as they, or, even more significantly, need a place to meet actively with study groups, tutors, and classmates. Academic libraries that have built a large number of group studies in a new or renovated facility often are very happy about the use that they receive, if not the abuse. If students still need a central information services facility and a place to interact with those services, then physical information resources should be accessible there as well. Many of the same arguments apply to the development of separate departmental libraries. If the mission of the academic library is to bring together the otherwise disparate disciplines and to encourage cross-disciplinary research and cross-fertilization of information, it seems to be a step in the wrong direction to balkanize the library collection over the range of academic departments at the university. The exceptions to this rule that seem to have worked are those that respond to clear, practical imperatives, such as a very large and dispersed university campus, or those planned with secure extra funding for duplicated staff and services in the branch location.   J. CLEMMER

Public Libraries

A problem encountered in many older libraries today is that the efficient expansion of the building is very difficult. Either the design of the building, multilevels, or partitioning and bearing walls make addition of new, more flexible use space very expensive and, in some cases, impossible. Expansion is also hindered by the unavailability of appropriate adjacent portions of the site that would provide adequate and efficient space for expansion. The potential for expanding the building currently being planned should be examined in each library building project. What alternatives are there to expanding the existing library? One alternative might be to build another series of libraries at a more distant part of the service area. But, expansion of the product, particularly when there are only ten to twenty years of growth in a library, does need to be part of the initial assessment of need.   D. SMITH

Access and Use
Public Libraries

In many metropolitan suburban areas, the typical library user has become very knowledgeable and sophisticated about where the desired library resources are housed. Library patrons typically will make use of two or three or sometimes more library facilities in the course of a week. They will go to one library for information of a popular nature, another library for special collections in the area of business materials, and perhaps a third library that may have some unique periodical or audiovisual or other resource that is limited in quantity to a few locations. The traditional branch and central library concept has diminished, particularly in growing metropolitan areas where branch libraries are assuming the mantle of pseudo-central libraries and are being described as area libraries or regional libraries.

2. David Kaser, "Twenty-five Years of Academic Library Building Planning," *College & Research Libraries* 45 (July 1984): 268–81.

There is some question in the literature now as to what a regional library is. Is it a 15,000-square-foot building with a slightly larger collection or is it a 30,000- or 80,000-square-foot branch library that has a much larger enhanced collection, a multiplicity of electronic data sources, a cable television studio, and a performing arts center? A dilemma in the case of many central cities is the degree to which they can support the flagship central library and its almost-research-library capacities and low user traffic and, at the same time, maintain the abundant traditional branch library structures, which in the days of the pedestrian were supposedly located within a mile or so of each household in the city. This problem has presented some very difficult planning issues for these particular cities.

Access has become less an issue concerning pedestrians and public transportation and more one of tying library use to access by private vehicle. A long-term issue will be the need for planning libraries with huge parking lots to accommodate users in order to make going to the library as easy as going to the local shopping mall. Libraries, therefore, share many of the same problems as commercial developments in making the library as visible and as accessible as its commercial counterparts.

Access also extends to the use of the building and how people can get in and out and through and around the building. We have been faced over almost two decades with serious and growing regulatory requirements in the area of access to libraries by the disabled and handicapped. Some planners who have been involved in library buildings for some time have gone through several permutations of regulations, all of which have become more restrictive. Restrooms that may have met the handicapped access requirements of the 1970s have suddenly become too small or inappropriately laid out in the 1980s. With the new Americans with Disabilities Act (Public Law 101-336) that was just passed will come the need in some institutions to redo facilities that, in fact, previously measured up to handicapped access requirements. Consultants, architects, and those involved in planning new facilities now should be on a speaking acquaintanceship with the publications issued by the federal government regarding the new Americans with Disabilities Act.

An additional point regarding aisle spacing concerns the now popular role of many libraries in providing browsing public collections. For browsing, a 36-inch aisle, particularly with long stack ranges, is very restrictive in terms of two-lane traffic of individuals. Although 36 inches may be a legal requirement, in this particular case it is a minimum that should be exceeded if a library is in fact going from traditional stack storage for collections to actual display of materials in the encouragement of the browser. If a library is going to take the latter role, it needs to invest in some additional building space, both as a result of reducing the length of the ranges and of spreading the ranges farther apart. Realistically, therefore, aisle spacing between shelving sections should be 42–48 inches.

The other part of this whole access question involves height of shelving. Typically, libraries that are trying to incorporate as many materials as possible into as small an area as possible have 90-inch-high shelving. Utilizing this shelving again in a browsing library where people are going to be looking through a full range of shelves rather than searching for a specific title will require reducing the shelving height to 84 inches or, in some libraries, down to 66–72 inches. As libraries reduce the numbers of shelves available, the space requirement increases. For example, if instead of stacking seven shelves the library wants to use only six in a specific collection section, approximately 15 percent more floor area must be provided to accommodate the necessary shelving. So access takes a variety of forms in terms of space available to house the collection adequately, space for circulating, space around seating in conjunction with service desks and, certainly in the stack areas, space to facilitate user ease of access.   D. SMITH

Academic Libraries

Regarding the theme of individual libraries relating to each other, much of what has been said about the distribution of public libraries and resources applies to networking of academic libraries as a whole. Such networking applies less to intracampus libraries and more to intercampus libraries in which academic libraries join to coordinate their services and collections over a wide geographic area. This cooperation often occurs in the context of sharing the purchase and operation of an automated system. Does this trend have significant architectural implications for the design of the individual campus library? This is apparently not the case so far. The basic elements per campus library probably will still be present even if one is networking to other libraries. The character of the collections within an individual institution's library in such a sharing arrangement would certainly be different. The architectural physical requirements of that collection may not change that much.

Regarding user spaces in the library, some substantial changes will be taking place in the near future. Brandeis University, for example, recently did away with the traditional reference desk altogether in favor of an information desk staffed only by graduate students. They built a new service point called a *research consultation office*, where users find reference librarians, generally on an appointment basis. An article about the experience will soon be published by Virginia Massey-Burzio, possibly within the next twelve months. The Brandeis experience may be a sign of future developments and certainly would carry strong implications for public services design.

For detailed information on regulations for disabled access to libraries, see the *Federal Register* of Tuesday, January 22, 1991. It carries the recommended accessibility guidelines of the U.S. Architectural and Transportation Barriers Compliance Board (*see* fig. 1). These guidelines are under consideration right now by the Department of Justice as possible criteria for their interpretation of the Rehabilitation Act of 1973. The comment period for these proposed guidelines passed on March 25, but the Department of Justice will not be issuing its final regulations until July 26. The guidelines cover the permissible height of at least a portion of service counters (28–34 inches), the permissible height of card catalog cabinets (54 inches), and the percentage of study carrels adapted to handicapped use (5 percent of the total). Perhaps with the strongest implication for overall layout of libraries, the guidelines recommend stack aisles be at least 36 inches wide, with 42 inches preferred. Many academic libraries have been designed to a few inches less than this. It is unclear at the moment as to how strongly that 36-inches requirement will be enforced. Fulfillment of the ideal would not leave adequate space in other parts of the library for staff and user services with the project dollars available. That often leads to a compromise of the 36-inch aisle width, with the understanding that in many academic collections the traffic through those aisles will not be so constant and voluminous as in a public library. Thus, many academic libraries have decided to feel comfortable with 32–33 inches in the stack aisle space.

Personnel coverage for access and use is also heavily affected by regulatory trends in fire protection. Experts in this field continue to urge librarians to accept sprinkling throughout the building, including

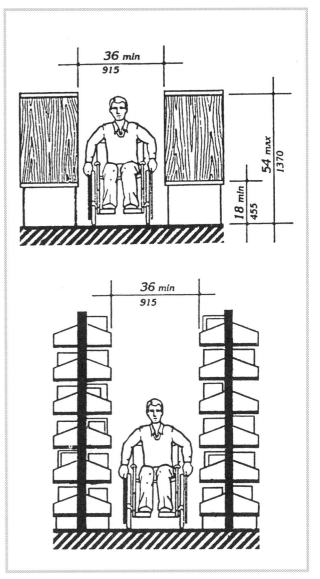

Figure 1. Examples of Accessibility Guidelines Recommended by the U.S. Architectural and Transportation Barriers Compliance Board
Source: *Federal Register* 58 (Jan. 22, 1991): 2383.

over collections.[3] A long and complex debate can be summarized by saying that more librarians are accepting that point of view for the following reasons:

1. the devastating experience of unsprinkled collections in fires; for example, that of the Los Angeles Public Library in 1986;
2. the proven effectiveness of freezing or freeze-drying procedures;

---

3. National Fire Protection Association, *Protection of Libraries and Library Collections*, NFPA 910 (Quincy, Mass.: The Association, 1985).

3. the development of dry head sprinklers;

4. the possibility of avoiding the damage caused by large-volume firehoses by using zoned sprinklers; and

5. the greater freedom of architectural design afforded by the life safety code to libraries with sprinklers.[4]   J. CLEMMER

Collection Resources
Academic Libraries

The design of academic library stack areas appears to be moving in the direction of economy. Considerations of cost-effectiveness and measurement of actual use have led to consideration of economizing space in the stack collections. Lieberfeld offers a particularly radical and trenchant opinion. Compact shelving has grown increasingly popular.[5] Cost-effectiveness studies by researchers such as Michael D. Cooper of Berkeley show that the ideal pattern of collection housing in the future may be a regional hierarchy of facilities.[6] The local collection of materials with proven high use might be supplemented by an on-campus, compact, open stack building. The latter would place lesser-used materials in a facility of low construction and moderate per-circulation costs. Finally, there might be regional cooperative storage of least-used materials in a facility of rock-bottom construction costs, albeit high per-circulation costs because of communication and transportation.

It may be true that it is not necessary to build quite as much shelving space for a given building lifespan as was formerly the case. Evidence for this proposition is provided by economic trends and the growing acceptance of high-density shelving.

The standard economic rules of thumb for academic library collection growth is the post–World War II era had collections doubling every sixteen years by devoting 30 percent of budgets to acquisitions. That rule is being broken. Recent research by Richard Werking, formerly of Trinity University and now of the Naval Academy Library, shows that between 1967 and 1987 three-quarters of selective college libraries and one-half of the Association for Research Libraries (ARL) libraries failed to double in size in spite of 40 percent budget expenditures for acquisitions by colleges and 35 percent by ARL libraries.[7] College libraries have been able, until recently, to increase expenditures for materials as a percentage of total expenditures in an attempt to chase inflation, but

ARL libraries were unable to do so. Latest reports are that the serials pricing crisis probably has overtaken that effort and most libraries now are cutting back. State-supported collegiate libraries often are faring even worse. The Minnesota State University and Community College System reported a 14 percent decline in expenditures for books (in constant dollars) between 1979 and 1988, while enrollments increased 20 percent.

As acquisitions budgets decline, budgets for "other" expenditures have gone from the 10 percent rule of thumb to 20 percent in selective colleges and 15 percent in ARL libraries.[8] Presumably this money is going for maintenance and related expenses of library automation, if not the initial capitalization. It is doubtful that libraries will recover the "double every sixteen years" pattern of forty years ago and this change should have implications for facility design.

There has been an increased public acceptance of compact shelving in recent years. Until the 1980s, librarians considered publicly accessible compact shelving in academic libraries with great trepidation. The huge installation at the University of Illinois library, however, proved that it is an acceptable alternative in an academic library. Again, economics plays a role. Studies by Cooper and others have shown the cost-effectiveness of high-density storage. Even relatively high-density, on-campus, fixed shelving, such as the storage building recently constructed at Southern Illinois University, has proven very attractive economically at $45 per square foot.[9] Compact shelving has achieved acceptance by academic users and should not be ruled out for public access areas.   J. CLEMMER

Public Libraries

A dramatic difference between the academic libraries attempting to apportion 30 percent to 40 percent of

4. National Fire Protection Association, *Life Safety Code Handbook*, 4th ed. (Quincy, Mass.: The Association, 1988).

5. Lawrence Lieberfeld, "The Curious Case of the Library Building," *College & Research Libraries* 44 (July 1983): 277–82.

6. Michael D. Cooper, "A Cost Comparison of Alternating Book Storage Strategies," *Library Quarterly* 59 (July 1989): 239–60.

7. Richard Hume Werking, "Collection Growth and Expenditures in Academic Libraries: A Preliminary Inquiry," *College & Research Libraries* 52 (Jan. 1991): 5–23.

8. Ibid.

9. Kenneth G. Peterson, "New Storage Facility at Southern Illinois University," *College & Research Libraries News* 51 (Jan. 1990): 39–43.

their budgets for material and public libraries is that it is the rare public library that is spending even 20 percent of its total budget on library materials. It is more common to find in public libraries that the expenditures for library materials are in the 9 percent to 12 percent range. Many library systems with multiple agencies and heavy turnover in circulation and use do not plan for heavy warehousing of materials. Hennepin County Library in Minnesota, for example, had a materials collection in 1970 of approximately 1,200,000 items. The annual report for 1990 for that library shows approximately 1,200,000 items. The heavy use of this collection (annual per capita circulation is approximately thirteen items) and very heavy weeding of the collection keeps the library materials in balance. In fact, the collection is wearing out faster than it can be supplemented. This is not the case in many smaller libraries where use is far lighter and the need to acquire and house certain basic collections is stronger.

A frequent assumption made by library board members or city council representatives, when the square footage and its allocation for a new public library is made known, is that with new technology and the marvels of electronic storage, libraries could shrink significantly and therefore be much less expensive to both build and operate. Fortunately, most understand when it is carefully explained that the publishing of hardcover materials for general public consumption has in fact increased dramatically in recent years. The space requirements of public libraries, therefore, must take this into account along with the need to provide for all the new marvelous formats of materials that are being made available and that the public has demanded. It is no longer enough simply to buy a hard copy or two of a currently popular publication. It must soon be followed by paperback versions, audio recordings, and videos of the miniseries as it appears on television. The net effect is that, on a per capita basis to provide full access to varied collection formats, libraries need to be substantially larger than they were planned for even five to ten years ago.

The use of compact shelving is frequently mentioned as one space-efficient way to house materials. Its application in public libraries is limited, except for those large, more research-oriented libraries that must store materials that are necessary but not needed as a browseable collection. This limitation, coupled with the substantial cost for compact shelving, which may run from $700 to $1,100 per double-faced

section, makes it of relatively little use in a public library. The Atlanta Central Library has some semi-public areas with periodical or government document storage for those who are interested in seeing an operating application in a public library setting.

D. Smith

Staff Spaces
Academic Libraries

Discussion of trends and issues in design of staff spaces can be approached at two levels. On the one hand, one can look at the total net square feet assigned to staff as a proportion of the whole library building. On the other, one can utilize standards to cumulate square footage assigned to individual staff members' workstations and derive the total needed. At the earliest stages of the project, the first approach can be taken but should be followed up very quickly by the more detailed approach. Rather than discuss specific details, this section of the chapter will point out some overall issues. The first is to be aware of the recommended ACRL methodology for overall staff space sizing. That standard recommends that the space be one-eighth the total devoted to user seating and collection. Be aware also that that figure was downsized considerably in the latest edition. Second, planners should consider whether the library staff is viewed as a federation of functional units or as a team of the whole, in which informal immediate communication is critical. Exploration of this issue will determine the ideal arrangement of overall staff spaces within any particular library. Because of both size and mission, there may be a division on this question between large and small academic libraries.

One view sees staff work units relating to the rest of the organization largely through formal mechanisms, such as an electronic network. An individual technical services librarian's work, for instance, does not necessitate proximity to an online public access catalog (OPAC) cluster because the same information is available to him or her no matter where the workstation is located. Considerations along these lines have led to "offshoring" technical services departments to other floors, or even to other buildings.

The opposing design viewpoint emphasizes overall staff team building and intragroup dynamics. In spite of technological possibilities, staff areas planned under this viewpoint are contiguous to the extent possible. In this manner, both formal and informal communication between departments is fostered. This pattern often results in a design logjam on level one since that is where the reference staff needs to be. If the technical services staff follows, the available square feet are often insufficient.

Some basic viewpoints about the nature of library work also govern the design of individual workstations. There is frequently dichotomy between reference librarian spaces and technical services stations. Because reference staffs spend a portion of their workday in a highly visible public environment, and then often need private consultation space as a supplement, it is increasingly common to develop offices for them. Technical services staff, however, tend, on the average, to live constantly within a work flow. Communication tends to be with colleagues (as opposed to the general public) and more evenly distributed through the workday. The radical daily change in milieu common to reference staff is rare among technical services personnel. Workstations, often purposely oversized and shared, can work well in this environment.   J. CLEMMER

Public Libraries

A major issue in facility planning for staff in public libraries is that of making the best use possible of the existing staff and avoiding having to add additional staff whenever possible. This is particularly relevant when looking at buildings that go to more than one level, or that, because of the size of the floor plate, require additional service desks. It is estimated that over a twenty-year period, a building operation maintaining a full-service desk with one or two staff members may cost more than $1 million in operating expenses as costs inflate. An interesting phenomenon that occurs when building planning begins for a library of any size is that the present staff organization comes under scrutiny, and frequently the structuring of a new building results in the restructuring of the library staff. What began as a relatively simple building program planning exercise becomes a more involved organizational planning effort.

A common occurrence in libraries that are growing crowded and running out of space is that staff areas have become seriously compressed. Staff are operating cheek-to-jowl in back areas, distant parts of the building, and in some cases in portions of the public service floor totally unsuited to both efficient

staff operations and productive work. A frequent response to this condition is that everybody wants his or her own office space, which in public libraries is totally unnecessary. Those persons who have full-time duties requiring concentration and particularly the supervision of other staff members do need a room with a door that closes. However, much of the public service staff in the library will be working for the greater share of their day on public service desk activities or in a general support service workroom setting. The need to provide an adequate number of individual workstations, properly organized and oriented so that the work flow goes efficiently, is critical, as is the allocation of terminals. Are these terminals dedicated to a single purpose or can they be used for multiple tasks? Frequently the library employs a substantial number of part-time staff members who can share a station in the back area with each one having individual storage and personal space.

D. SMITH

Summary
Academic Libraries

Design solutions for a new or renovated academic library flow from a vision of the library now and in the future. The vision can be analyzed in terms of public, staff, and collection spaces. For each area there are a set of planning issues that each institution should answer for itself. This exercise is especially critical now that libraries entering a period of change to new forms of scholarly communication. Ideally, sufficient time will be allowed to engage the campus community in dialogue on these issues, a process that should be intellectually stimulating and give prominence to the library as an idea. Specific plans for each major area of the library are dependent on the campus community's answers to the following related broader issues:

1. The future role of the library in academic life must be defined in order to write overall building planning objectives.
2. A vision of how new information technologies will affect scholarly research and the future of publishing is needed in order to make informed decisions on collection spaces.
3. Public service areas can be specified only with an informed sense of how, where, and why students study, as well as their need for consultation and support.

4. Staff areas can be designed after defining the nature of library staff work in public and technical services and determining how library facility design will affect staff cooperation and communication.   J. CLEMMER

Public Libraries

Where are public libraries going in the next few years? According to a succinct article in *Library Journal* written by Linda Crismond when she was the Los Angeles County librarian, areas where libraries would see little change include the provision of books, a steady population growth, and a shortage of professional staff. Areas where libraries might want to initiate change include the improvement of services, the use of new technology, and the expansion of the present financial support base. Areas over which libraries have had no control include new formats of material, adaptation to new political environments, and the acceptance of greater entrepreneurship. The measure of success that can be applied to public libraries will be how well they respond to each of these three categories. Charles Robinson, Baltimore County librarian, sees the public libraries as "attempting to be the French restaurant of institutions rather than the McDonald's of information and materials distribution." The provision of public library facilities aimed at furnishing service to persons supporting the library is the ultimate objective from Robinson's perspective. What are some of the concerns librarians will need to address as they plan libraries for the 1990s and beyond?

1. *Facilitation of full self-utilization by the public.* Through signage, organization, layout, and design, the public should find libraries easy to use.

2. *Efficiency in staff utilization.* The reverse of the first item is that libraries will have to do more with fewer staff, and in many cases, more with lower-paid staff, so that the building must serve as the instrument to facilitate this economic requirement.

3. *Security for people, collections, and facilities.* Security within libraries will be an increasingly critical issue—security for users and staff, security for collections, and security of the building against fire and other destructive acts.

4. *Wise investment in technology.* Librarians will need to become much more knowledgeable in the practical applications of all that new technology affords and to make, in some cases, hard decisions as to what will or will not be included in libraries.

5. *Lighting and building environment.* Librarians will need to learn to deal with complicated issues, such as proper lighting for both the senior citizen with decreasing vision and the user requiring a non-glare computer screen. Planners will need to provide attractive space in buildings for both serious and leisure time use, as well as for all age groups. The use of energy will reappear as a major issue.

6. *More space, higher operating costs, lower budgets.* Planners will have to work even harder with decreasing dollars to provide as much space as possible to accommodate both the traditional services and the new opportunities that libraries are able to provide.

Andrew Carnegie felt that "the very best gift that could be given to a community" was a public library. That sentiment remains as true with the approach of the twenty-first century as it did at the start of the twentieth century.   D. SMITH

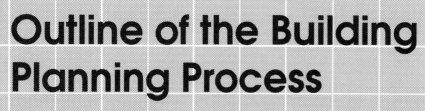

Outline of the Building Planning Process

or

An Overly Simplified Summary of What Will Be Visited upon You When You Build a Building

Anders Dahlgren

In trying to find some quotable story to begin with, I remembered three voices belonging to an unknown cartoonist, a former prime minister, and a Chinese philosopher. The cartoonist comes from the *New Yorker,* and the picture shows a Spanish conquistador with his aides-de-camp atop a hill along what would be for Europeans a virgin coast, the sun setting in magnificent splendor in the background as he waves his arm in a grand display and says: "Someday, this will all be *infrastructure!*" The prime minister is Winston Churchill, who says: "We shape our buildings; thereafter they shape us." And the philosopher is Lao Tze, who says: "The reality of a building is not to be found in the walls and roof, but in the space within."

These three sound bites have quite a bit to do with what makes the dynamics of planning library buildings exciting. We are, indeed, dealing with the infrastructure, and it is, as Edward T. Bear might say, a capital I-Important, capital T-Topic. The infrastructure, being what it is, does tend to create or limit the opportunities that we have to deliver library service to our clienteles, and the infrastructure, being what it is, is merely that which surrounds

and houses the service we seek to provide. Effective building design starts with an understanding of the services your library needs to provide, and, if done well, effective building design—well, I suppose it never really ends but it brings you to a place that will be continually responsive to the evolving service goals of your library.

So keeping these three assembled humorists in mind, let me go on to observe that most of us approach a library building project with a mixture of trepidation, anticipation, anxiety, dread, and excitement. It's a time of great challenge and momentous opportunity for any library; the decisions you make as you undertake your building project will affect your library's ability to deliver services through the coming generation, and even longer. And most of us, as we approach a building project, are unprepared.

The first time through, we find ourselves embarking on a new kind of project and we don't quite know what to expect. The next time, and the next, and the next, even knowing more of what to expect, we find that there are ample opportunities for surprise.

We need to note, by way of our continuing introduction and orientation, that the literature tries to help. There are a great many guides to the building planning process to be found in the literature, all of

Anders Dahlgren is a consultant for public library construction with the Wisconsin Division for Library Services in Madison.

them intended to offer up bearings, to provide the novice or experienced traveler with a sense of direction through these sometimes calm, sometimes turbulent waters. All of these guides are helpful, all of them offer useful insights, and all of them are a little bit wrong. If you take nothing else from this presentation it should be this:

Rule 1: No published description of the building planning process will resemble your planning process.

The published summaries are neat, tidy, and linear. Step one is followed by step two, is followed by step three, and the summaries make it all seem very easy and straightforward. But in the real world, you'll find, the process is rarely neat, tidy, and linear.

In fact, there is a corollary to Rule 1: The more detailed a published outline is, the more likely it is to be inaccurate.

Maybe the best outline I've seen was produced by Ray Holt for the first edition of the *Wisconsin Library Building Project Handbook,* in which five steps, or phases, are laid out:

Concept
Planning
Architectural implementation
Construction
Occupation

Keep this general framework in mind. Most of the outlines in the literature can be organized into these five phases. In fact, the *Building Project Handbook* itself starts with these five phases and goes on to embellish them into thirteen sub-steps (*see* fig. 1).

The concept phase involves the first two substeps: needs assessment and the evaluation of alternatives. Needs assessment, in the simplest terms, asks the question, how big a building do we need to meet the service demands of the community? It's a simple question requiring a complex response, and luckily subsequent chapters will address some of these complexities. Needs assessment evaluates current library service capabilities and the current conditions and limitations of the physical plant. Needs assessment also projects those needs into the future, as best our murky crystal balls will allow. In some ways, needs assessment establishes the library's long-range goals. It defines the playing field.

The second sub-step, the evaluation of alternatives, applies the findings of the needs assessment step in search of an implementation strategy. The needs assessment might suggest a variety of alternatives for

A. CONCEPT
   1. Needs Assessment
   2. Evaluation of Alternatives

B. PLANNING
   3. Writing a Building Program Statement
   4. Assembling the Project Team
   5. Selecting a Site
   6. Securing Financing

C. ARCHITECTURAL IMPLEMENTATION
   7. Developing a Plan for an Expanded Building
   8. Interior Design
   9. Plans Analysis

D. CONSTRUCTION
   10. Bidding and Contract Negotiation
   11. Construction

E. OCCUPATION
   12. Moving In
   13. Evaluation

Figure 1. Building Planning Process Outline
Source: Adapted from *Wisconsin Library Building Project Handbook.*

consideration, to meet the identified need. One might

1. reallocate space within the existing building, for example, converting unused storage space to "found" space for expanded collections,
2. place an addition on the existing building,
3. build a new building,
4. convert some other existing structure into a new library,
5. reconsider the library service goals and recast them in hopes of achieving some corresponding reduction in space need, or
6. do nothing in hopes that the need will go away.

Specific situations might suggest other solutions. The need for continued collection growth, for example, could be met by establishing an off-site storage facility for infrequently used materials. Each of these varied alternatives has advantages, some more than others, and each has disadvantages. In evaluation, the alternatives should be examined from the standpoint of effectiveness, cost, feasibility, and utility, among other topics.

The planning phase involves sub-steps 3, 4, 5,

and 6: writing a building program statement, assembling the project team, selecting a site, and securing financing.

Writing a building program statement more or less corresponds to the whole show. It is the key to success. Luckily, others are going to discuss the programming process and the mechanics of how you go about writing a program, so I can simply call the building program statement the library's instructions to an architect. Or, if you want a definition that you can jot down for your notes: A building program statement is "a practical description of the library's functional needs, based on its projected use and service goals."[1]

Assembling the project team, the fourth sub-step in this process, brings together the individuals and groups who will need to participate in and support the project in order to make it happen: the governing authority, the librarian, the architect, consultants of various ilks, the contractor, and so on. In the next chapter Bob Carmack writes about the "who does what" after I finish with the "what happens when," so I will leave those details to him.

Before you can presume to build, even before you can perpetrate a specific design solution, you have to know where you're going to build, and that is what site selection (sub-step 5) is about. The conventional wisdom regarding site selection holds that a library should be located on a site both accessible and visible to its clientele, with complementary uses in the surrounding vicinity. For public libraries, this conventional wisdom has translated traditionally into a site in the central business district, and while there are some indications that the conventional wisdom is starting to translate into something other than the central business district, the notions of accessibility, visibility, and compatible adjacent uses still apply.

Financing the project is offered here as the sixth sub-step, but it is one of the activities that doesn't often occur at one discrete point in the process. Fund-raising may get started much, much earlier, or it can get started later. Options for financing strategies may include public funding sources—tax appropriations, bond issues, state or federal grants. Options may also include private funding sources—solicitation of donors and bequests, coordinated fund-raising campaigns, and so on. Some combination of public and private sources may be employed. The needs assessment and facilities programming process, establishing goals and parameters for the project, and determining the scope and strategy for your building

expansion, will define the extent of fund-raising required, which in turn will suggest options and strategies.

The design phase includes sub-steps 7, 8, and 9: developing a plan for an expanded building, interior design, and plans analysis. Developing a plan refers to the architect's interpretation and translation into graphic form of the library's expression of its service goals and how a facility can best support those goals (i.e., the library's building program statement). An architect may first develop conceptual or relationship diagrams, which evolve into an initial, or schematic, design. The schematic design lays out interior and exterior doors and walls and windows, and provides enough information for other members of the planning team to assess whether sufficient space is devoted to the library's respective functions and whether all those spaces are arranged in a suitable and functional way. As the schematics are approved, the design phase moves into design development, a testing of engineering assumptions, and into the preparation of detailed working drawings and specifications.

Interior design (sub-step 8) usually overlaps with the development of an architectural plan. The structural plan and the furnishings plan must develop in tandem to ensure that they will coordinate, that ceilings are the right height for stacks and that outlets and lighting fixtures are placed where they will be needed. Existing furniture to be retained and moved from the old building to the new will be identified; new furnishings to be acquired will be selected.

Plans analysis is the ninth sub-step, and in practice it runs parallel with the various architectural design steps and beyond. Consider plans analysis as an opportunity to test the architect's and interior designer's plans to confirm that they meet the library's programmatic and service requirements. The program calls for X sections of shelving: are there X sections of shelving in the plan? The program calls for periodical backfiles in close proximity to the indexes: is it shown on the plan? The program calls for indirect lighting throughout: is it so on the plan? The program calls for electrical and data transmission support at every staff workstation: is it so? Obviously, this review is part of every step of the architectural implementation phase, and it continues

1. Anders Dahlgren, *Planning the Small Public Library Building*, Small Libraries Publications, no. 11 (Chicago: American Library Association, 1985) 6.

into construction when you may be called upon to consider changes to the original plans.

The construction phase includes sub-steps 10 and 11: bidding and contract negotiation and construction.

Bidding and contract negotiation is the sub-step that adds the builder/contractor to the project roster. For many projects, the bidding and negotiation phase involves the solicitation of bids, the invitation of prospective builders to review the approved plans and specifications and to submit an estimate of the cost to build the building as proposed in the plans. Usually, state and federal laws will govern bidding activities.

Construction is the eleventh sub-step of the process outlined in the *Wisconsin Library Building Project Handbook*, and maybe everyone is far enough removed from the actual digging and mud and muck of building that we can just say that the building goes up, no problem, which leads us directly to the occupation phase, which wraps things up with the last two sub-steps: moving in and evaluation.

When you move into the building, it will be on a sunny day, and just like the construction phase, it will go smoothly because you've planned it all so well and hired the most qualified and capable movers to help you with the job. If this is possible, the dedication will be held on an even sunnier day, crowds will come out and bands will play, stirring speeches will be made, and you'll feel a well-earned sense of pride in your accomplishment.

Evaluation is the final sub-step in this particular sequence, and it is a step that's frequently overlooked. After you move into the new building, it's all too easy to revert to directing a library, or doing other actual library things, and to put behind you the diversion of running a construction project. You may be inclined to let the building take care of itself, while you make yourself into a librarian once again. But, in a spirit of closure, it is important to assess whether your building project met its goals. After you have settled into the building, invite the architect and other members of the planning team back to ask, Did the project in fact meet its goals? Does the building perform as expected? What changes have been made to adapt to unforeseen use patterns? Are further changes needed? What elements work just as intended?

That's one outline of what happens when one is involved in a building project. Here's another variation on this theme. Anders' Ten Quick and Dirty Surefire Steps to an Expanded Building (*see* fig. 2) includes these steps:

> Literature review/self-education
> Needs assessment
> Building program statement
> Architect selection
> Site selection
> Schematic design
> Design development
> Bidding and negotiation
> Construction
> Moving in and dedication

You can see that the Ten Quick and Dirty Surefire Steps correspond more or less to the thirteen sub-steps we've just gone over. They add a step called "Literature review/self-education" at the outset, encouraging you to attend preconferences like this one and to read through some of the basic sources in the literature to become familiar with basic space planning issues. It's not a difficult subject, but it is unfamiliar, and when you're facing the process for the first time (or the second or third or fourth), you'll benefit from every bit of background you can assemble. The Ten Quick and Dirty Surefire Steps also combine needs assessment and evaluation into a single step, pass off selecting the architect as assembling the larger building team, and more or less ignore financing. They collapse interior design and plans analysis into the design development step, and they don't say much at all about post-occupancy evaluation. Of course, the Ten Quick and Dirty Steps do list separate steps for schematic design and design development, instead of the one-step, "developing a plan."

Or, if you want an outline of the process that's almost sure to be different from your process, look at the twenty-two steps that Charles Reid and I dispatched for an article on facilities planning for the latest edition of Virginia Young's *The Library Trustee* (*see* fig. 3). The twenty-two steps took the guise of responsibilities that a public library board will have in a library construction project, but they are laid out in an order fashioned roughly after the general planning process. And that's pretty much a guarantee your project won't happen that way. If you consider these steps, whether the ten quick and dirty ones or the thirteen, or the twenty-two, it should become obvious that the process may not unfold in this simple, linear fashion.

Maybe site selection will be the first step in your

The Library Building Planning Team:
Who Does What When?

The following ten steps provide a brief description of the process involved with planning a new or expanded library facility. On the right side of the page, key members of the library planning team are listed and their relative involvement in each step is noted (the more +s, the greater the typical level of involvement; a * means the level of involvement may vary, depending on local circumstances). Be aware that the chart is only representative; there are as many variations on these themes as there are libraries and potential building projects.

The building consultant is an optional, though oftentimes recommended, component of the planning team. If one is retained, the consultant will probably be more closely involved in the project's early planning stages. Likewise, the architect's involvement in early program planning may vary depending on the library's preferences as well as when in the process the architect is retained.

The far right column is used to note steps when others may become involved with the project (e.g., when it may be important to seek the endorsement of the library's governing authority, or review by legal counsel).

Facilities Planning: Ten Steps	Board	Libn	Arch	Cons	Others
1. Literature review/self education Library board and staff familiarize themselves with basic issues and concepts in library space planning.	+ +	+ + +			
2. Needs assessment Projecting the community's service requirements into the future, the library's long-term needs are identified; needs assessment provides an initial answer to the important question: "How big?"	+ +	+ + +		+ + +	
About funding Project costs are budgeted during these stages, and funding alternatives explored; implementation of the funding strategy may continue through construction.					
3. Building program statement The library's space needs are described in as much detail as time and talents allow; the building program describes the overall space need, classifies the need into functional departments or areas, and describes optimum interrelationships among areas.	+ +	+ + +		+ + +	Municipal endorsement
4. Architect selection The board selects the design professional who will translate the library's written expression of need into a plan for an expanded facility.	+ + +	+ +	+	*	Legal review of architect's contract

Figure 2. The Library Building Planning Team: Who Does What When?
Source: *The Library Trustee: A Practical Guidebook*, 2nd ed., ed. Virginia G. Young (Chicago: American Library Association, 1988).

	Board	Libn	Arch	Cons	Others
5. Site selection The site should be large enough to support the expanded facility as well as on-site parking requirements of the municipality; it should allow for future expansion; it should meet crucial recommendations regarding accessibility and visibility.	+ + +	+ +	*	*	Legal review of purchase contract Municipal approval?
6. Schematic design Working from the building program statement, the architect develops a preliminary design outlining the location of basic structural elements—walls, doors, windows, and so on; the staff reviews the functional implications of the design; the board approves the final schematic.	+	+ +	+ + +	*	Review by municipal planning or zoning commission?
7. Design development The architect expands upon the preliminary design, filling in engineering and other technical details; at the end of this process, the board approves the completed working drawings for submission to bidders.	+	+ +	+ + +	*	Interior designer Legal review of working drawings (esp. general and supplementary conditions) Municipal approval?
8. Bidding and negotiation In accordance with applicable federal, state, and local procurement regulations, contractors are invited to bid on the project described in the working drawings; bids are opened, and after negotiations, a contract is signed.	+ + +	+ +	+ + +	*	Legal review of process, bids, contract Municipal approval?
9. Construction The contractor(s) builds the new structure or addition as instructed by the working drawings; the architect typically monitors construction as the library's official representative; the librarian assists with monitoring; the board reserves the authority to approve payouts and changes to the contract.	+	+ +	+ + +	*	Contractor(s) on site as needed Building inspectors Legal review of payouts, change orders
10. Moving in and dedication The celebration of a challenging and rewarding accomplishment.	+ + +	+ + +			

1. Select a qualified librarian (if one is not already employed) to direct the service planning to be reflected in the building program.
2. Study the community, including broad demographic, economic, and other trends as they define library service needs.
3. Initiate a needs assessment based on the community study.
4. Consider the alternatives to meeting the needs: rental property, an addition, a new building, etc. If the decision is to construct a new building or an addition, the ensuing steps need to be taken.
5. Select and appoint a qualified building consultant.
6. Evolve and approve a written building program statement describing present and future building needs.
7. Appoint a building committee from within the board membership, or, if the board membership is small enough, the board can act as a committee of the whole.
8. Plan and direct a campaign to let the community know about the need for new or expanded facilities.
9. Select and appoint an attorney.
10. If the project is not endowed, plan and conduct a referendum campaign or whatever is needed financially.
11. Select and appoint a qualified architect.
12. Select and purchase a site with the advice and assistance of the planning team.
13. Approve preliminary plans.
14. Estimate the cost of operating the new building and seek assurance of adequate operating funds once the building is completed.
15. Approve the final plans and authorize the invitation for bids.
16. Approve construction contracts.
17. Monitor project progress.
18. Select and appoint an interiors specialist.
19. Approve furniture and equipment contracts.
20. Approve and pay invoices.
21. Arrange the dedication and open house.
22. Help to acquaint the public with the new services and programs now possible and available.

Figure 3. 22 Surefire Steps to an Expanded Library Facility (public library variation)

Source: *The Library Trustee: A Practical Guidebook*, 2nd ed., ed. Virginia G. Young (Chicago: American Library Association, 1988).

process. One of the first building projects I was ever involved with received its first boost when a couple of downtown parcels came on the market, parcels that the municipality had identified as a possible site for a new library building; and when they became available, the city contacted the library and wondered whether we ought to buy that land. We did backtrack, of course, and hurriedly assessed our needs and started to develop a building program statement, because we wanted to be sure that the site was in fact large enough to support a building of the size needed. The property was purchased in pretty short order.

In other cases site selection is a step with which you won't be bothered. It may be political suicide to suggest moving from the library's present location. Or it may be that past generations of wise planners had graced the library with a well-situated location on a site with ample room for an addition. In either instance, site selection may be a step that need not receive much attention.

Or, as was noted before, fund-raising may start early. Or it may start late. Or the architect has already, in effect, been selected, because the original building was done by Firm XYZ and everyone had such a good experience that they want to continue working with these folks. Or there are other nits to pick. Architects have critiqued the Ten Quick and Dirty Surefire Steps for consolidating their design development step and construction documents step into a single step. They point out, and rightly so, that schematic design is one step, followed by design development wherein the schematics are refined and mechanical and structural assumptions are tested, and after that an architect launches into the preparation of working drawings, the detailed plans from which the building will be built. True enough, and the critique is understandable, since design is an architect's work, it's their product, and this distinction is crucial to them. Unfortunately Eleven Quick and Dirty Steps doesn't have quite the same ring as Ten Quick and Dirty Steps.

There are many variations on this theme, all of them with merit, and none of them to be followed too closely. The planning process is usually a much more fluid process than what is described in the literature, and I'd like to try and move us away from these somewhat artificial summaries and toward something a little less linear.

"The Library Building Game" (*see* fig. 4) is included for two reasons: first, it describes a building planning process that allows for options, even mistakes;

and second, it takes the form of a game. Here's hoping it will be a continuous reminder for you that planning and building an expanded library *can be fun*. You *will* be having fun. Remember that.

"The Library Building Game" plays like an actual game. The instructions tell you to start at the beginning; sometimes it's tempting to start elsewhere, but the building game is best played from the beginning. To play the game, move forward one space or two spaces at a time, depending on the toss of a die or coin. Call heads a one-step move, tails a two-step move. Your direction is determined by the arrows printed on the board. The only other rule is that if your turn ends in a square with two arrows leading from it, your next move will follow the vertical arrow, either up or down; but if your first step in a two-square move is into a square with two arrows leading from it, you will follow the horizontal arrow, to the left or right.

Doesn't it sound like fun already? So, start in the upper left-hand corner in the square labeled Start Here, the square that quotes Bette Davis from *All about Eve*: "Fasten your seat belts, it's gonna be a bumpy night." Next, flip a coin. If it is heads, advance one square; if it is tails, advance two squares, etc., until you reach the end.

Following is a sample scenario: After you've evaluated options and costs, your next turn may have you presenting the alternatives to a wildly supportive funding authority. Or the funding authorities may be reluctant to authorize the project as proposed and you're sent back a few squares to redo the space needs assessment. And as you follow through the rest of the game, you'll see that you select a site, you draft a building program statement, and select an architect. Over here, if the toss of the coin doesn't go in your favor you can get caught in the endless fund-raising loop. There's design development and the authorization to solicit bids. Maybe the bids come in way over budget and you lose a turn and go through a redesign to scale the project back to reduce costs; or maybe the bids come in at or below the budget and you schedule the groundbreaking ceremony for a sunny day. Construction begins, excavation and foundation work are completed. Here, a natural disaster of epic proportions brings work at the job site to a standstill; you lose a turn. The building goes up, and the roof goes on. All the while you're avoiding the Dread Black Hole of Poor Planning. OOOOOOPS! A strike called by the building trade of your choice slows progress; you lose another turn.

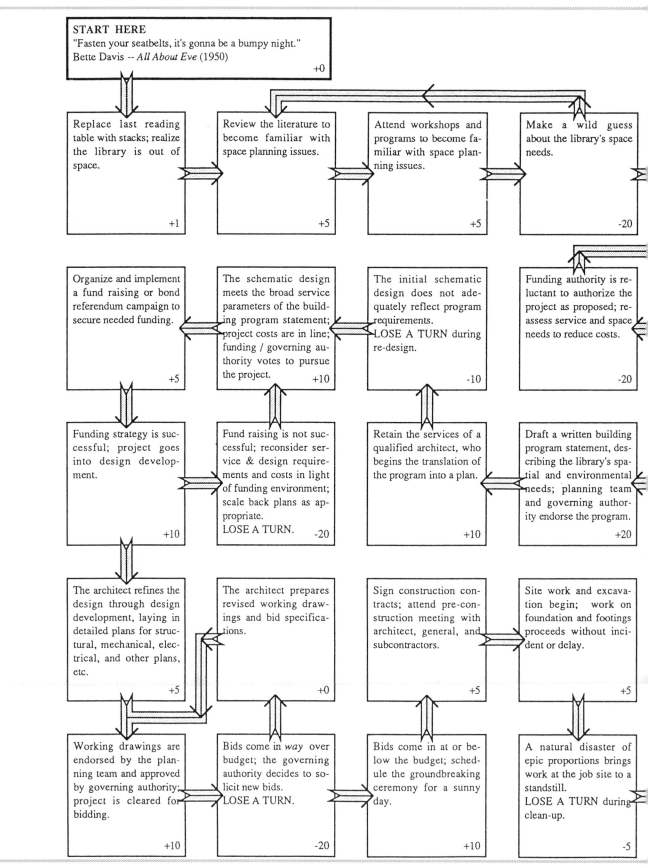

Figure 4. The Library Building Game

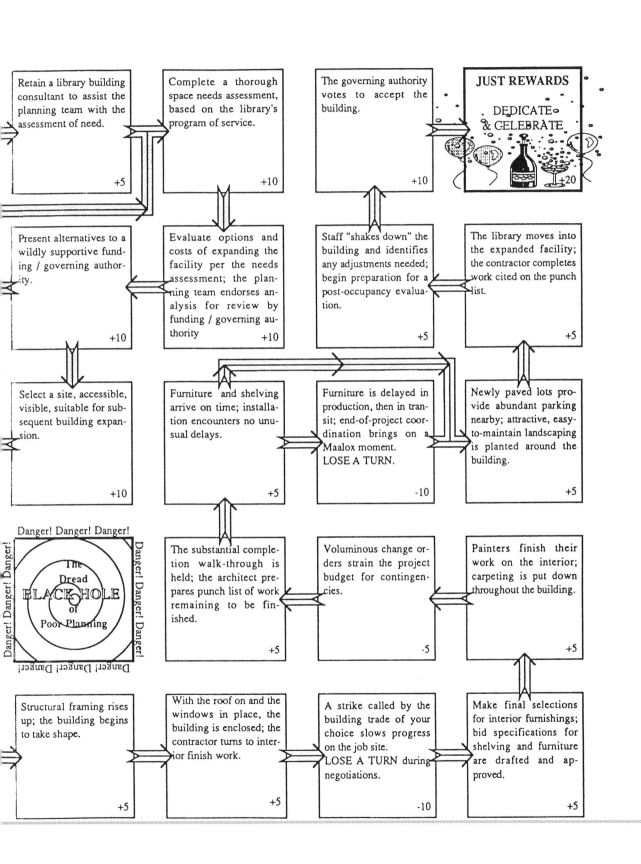

Retain a library building consultant to assist the planning team with the assessment of need.

+5

Complete a thorough space needs assessment, based on the library's program of service.

+10

The governing authority votes to accept the building.

+10

JUST REWARDS

DEDICATE & CELEBRATE

+20

Present alternatives to a wildly supportive funding / governing authority.

+10

Evaluate options and costs of expanding the facility per the needs assessment; the planning team endorses analysis for review by funding / governing authority

+10

Staff "shakes down" the building and identifies any adjustments needed; begin preparation for a post-occupancy evaluation.

+5

The library moves into the expanded facility; the contractor completes work cited on the punch list.

+5

Select a site, accessible, visible, suitable for subsequent building expansion.

+10

Furniture and shelving arrive on time; installation encounters no unusual delays.

+5

Furniture is delayed in production, then in transit; end-of-project coordination brings on a Maalox moment.
LOSE A TURN.

-10

Newly paved lots provide abundant parking nearby; attractive, easy-to-maintain landscaping is planted around the building.

+5

Danger! Danger! Danger!

The Dread BLACK HOLE of Poor Planning

Danger! Danger! Danger!

The substantial completion walk-through is held; the architect prepares punch list of work remaining to be finished.

+5

Voluminous change orders strain the project budget for contingencies.

-5

Painters finish their work on the interior; carpeting is put down throughout the building.

+5

Structural framing rises up; the building begins to take shape.

+5

With the roof on and the windows in place, the building is enclosed; the contractor turns to interior finish work.

+5

A strike called by the building trade of your choice slows progress on the job site.
LOSE A TURN during negotiations.

-10

Make final selections for interior furnishings; bid specifications for shelving and furniture are drafted and approved.

+5

Furniture is selected and bid. Finish work on the interiors proceeds. Maybe voluminous change orders strain the project budget for contingencies. You have a substantial completion walkthrough. Look: Furniture and shelving arrive on time; installation encounters no unusual delays! Or maybe it's: Furniture is delayed in production, then in transit; end-of-project coordination brings on a Maalox moment.

And so you move in, you shake down the building, you begin preparations for the post-occupancy evaluation, and the governing authority votes to accept the building. You dedicate the building and celebrate the accomplishments. One way or another, though, you can and will get through the process. It's challenging, sometimes even trying, but it's eminently survivable. You'll probably encounter setbacks, you'll probably be turned back a few squares sometimes, and you may even be sent back to square one. But with persistence, careful planning, and a sure implementation, you can win "The Library Building Game." And you can have fun doing it.

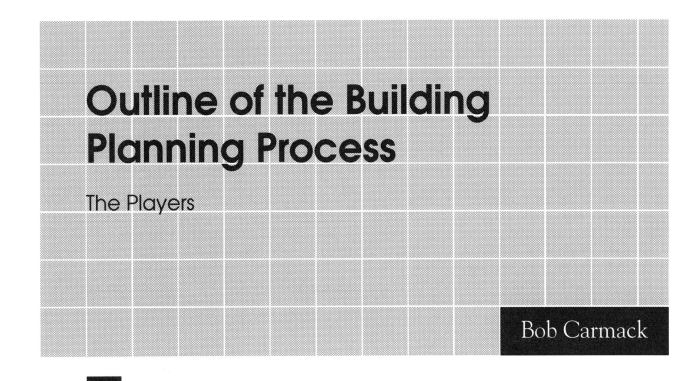

Outline of the Building Planning Process

The Players

Bob Carmack

Few, if any, other projects are going to be as important in your professional library career as building a library building. The decisions you make in planning and constructing a building are going to be around to either honor you or haunt you for a long time to come. Therefore, it behooves any librarian getting involved in a building project to surround himself or herself with the best help he or she can get in planning the building. Planning a building is a complex process and outside of a few folks I know—like Ray Holt, David Kaser, Nancy McAdams, Bob Rohlf, and Anders Dahlgren, to name a few—no one librarian can build a successful building by himself or herself. It has to be a team effort if it is going to be successful! The successful team will bring together a group of committed folks who have a variety of backgrounds, skills, and capabilities. Blending these talents into a working, cohesive group will be a challenge but it must be done.

Who are the some of the players? Briefly stated, they are the librarian, the governing body, staff, users, consultant(s), architect, design specialists, and others such as attorneys, facilities planners, and friends of the library. The key players are the librarian,

the governance authority, the library building consultant, the architect, and the contractor.

Before we take a closer look at the role of some of these players, let me emphasize getting to know the literature by making a few suggestions. Gloria Novak's piece, "Planning Teams for Library Building Projects," in *Planning Library Buildings: From Decision to Design* (LAMA, 1986), is a particularly cogent look at the involvement of various players in the process. Virginia Young's *The Library Trustee* (ALA, 1988) has useful information for the public library board while the revised text of Keyes Metcalf's *Planning Academic and Research Library Buildings* (ALA, 1986) is helpful for the academic librarian. Ray Holt has contributed significantly to the literature, but his latest book, *Planning Library Buildings and Facilities: From Concept to Completion*, synthesizes his vast knowledge into one source. Holt and Anders Dahlgren's *Wisconsin Library Building Project Handbook* is also filled with pithy hints for success. Dahlgren has also written ALA's *Planning the Small Public Library Building* (ALA, 1985) as well as edited a theme issue on library buildings for the fall 1987 issue of *Library Trends*.

Novak's piece in *Planning Library Buildings: From Decision to Design*, where she defines the three phases of a building project and the teams necessary to

---

Bob Carmack is the director of the University of Wisconsin Library in Superior.

provide appropriate information and action, is an excellent introduction to the roles and variety of needs to be accomplished by the participants. Novak emphasizes the importance of having a broad mix of expertise, skills, and power involved in planning a project. Remember that a building project is as much a political decision as it is a fiscal one, and many groups need to be involved to insure, if nothing else, appropriate communication and advice so that the project is a success.

Let me begin my discussion of the players by sharing with you my perceptions of the role of the librarian. I've often wished that every librarian could have the privilege and experience of planning and building a new library. In few other projects that you become involved with are you apt to experience the spectrum of human emotions or test all of the learning you acquired, either on the job or in library school, than working on a building project. It can be exhilarating, it can be frustrating, it can be fun, and it can be maddening. I guarantee that once you've done one there will be few other problems or crises in your positions that you won't be able to deal with. In a building project you'll have gotten a firsthand primer in politics, diplomacy, egos, finances, standards, design, collaboration, cooperation, co-opting, and communication, to name only a few. Though ostensibly the governing board will be the front for all of this, in reality, more often than not, the plain old scut work is going to have to be done by you.

You, the librarian, become the focal point in making the project go. By design or by default, you will be doing most of the work. You will have convinced the appropriate persons in the governance structure that a building need exists. You will have read the books, reviewed the literature, and developed a level of expertise that will enable you to successfully lead the project. You will represent and provide the local expertise. You will have to be responsible for taking the need statement beyond what Anders Dahlgren refers to, in his library building game, as "wild guessing." You'll be involved in the drafting of the program statement, authorizing and selling the project, both internally and externally, as well as serving as project director once the project is underway, unless you have the luxury of a facilities planner on your staff. You will have to learn to be a master politician, diplomat, psychologist, trouble-shooter, crisis manager, and communicator, among other things, in order to accomplish the project. As the representative of your governing entity, either directly or indirectly, you will be expected to be hard-nosed and to manage the project responsibly (translated, know how to say no). Unfortunately, if the building is a bomb, you will have to live with the results. Conversely, if it's a roaring success you may not receive the accolades that you richly deserve. Regardless, it really is a fun thing to "do" a building, if for no other reason than not everyone gets to do one and, more often than not, the results are worth the effort.

The makeup of the teams that will work throughout the process should not be left to chance. The librarian should take a leadership role in forming the teams that will work throughout the project. In many cases, the librarian will not be able to appoint anyone formally. That authority will usually rest with the governing board. However, the librarian should make recommendations or submit a list of nominees for membership and be prepared to be influential in the appointment process. The usefulness of each person nominated for involvement in the project needs to be carefully considered before the appointments are made. It would not serve anyone's purpose well at all if persons were appointed who had axes to grind, hobbies to pursue, and were not reflective of the community's interest at large. It's crucial that the right blend of background, experience, and ability to make things happen be represented in the project-planning infrastructure. Each librarian should learn the politics of the selection process and make it work for him or her.

Let me turn now to the governing board and its activities. In most public libraries, the boards of trustees will make the decisions. In academic settings, most schools will have their own board of trustees for such decision making with variations in structure dependent, usually, upon sources of funding. The boards of private academic institutions will resemble the public library board in terms of their makeup, i.e., a judicious blend of interests, experiences, and influences, though their membership may be more geographically dispersed. Boards of state-assisted colleges and universities may serve a larger forum with responsibilities delegated back to the local level. In any case there is a group of laypersons, appointed for their own particular interests and usefulness, who will make decisions that impact on your building process. From this group will evolve the overall authority and responsibility for the building project.

The role of the library board in a building project

is very well delineated in Young's *The Library Trustee* and Holt and Dahlgren's *Wisconsin Library Building Project Handbook,* so really there is little use for me to be expansive here. Let me say though, that even though they are written primarily for the benefit of public library boards of trustees, this list can, with few exceptions, be adapted to serve academic and special library settings. All that is needed is a broad interpretation of some of the phrases, e.g., the community.

In summary, and briefly stated, the major responsibilities of the governing board include, but are not limited to, making decisions, appointing the planning teams, assisting in the politics of getting the library project sold and funded, hiring architects and consultants, and not making the librarian's life miserable as that person gets the building built.

Let's turn now to involvement of the staff in a building project. I mentioned just a while back that a building is as much a political decision as it is a fiscal consideration. Politically, in this day of shared governance, to use an academic term, building a library building without involving the library staff in a meaningful way is sheer folly. In all but the smallest libraries there is going to exist a cadre of talent, expertise, and experience that will be useful to the project. This expertise and experience can be useful in the fact-finding process, in the development of the program statement, in the selling of the project, and in public relations. Remember, for many of these folks, the library is their life and their future, and they deserve to have some say in their own destiny. Wise planners and leaders will not overlook the wisdom that resides within the library staff.

Let me digress here to describe a particularly neat way for involving the staff in a building project that I experienced just recently while serving as a member of the building design team for a new public library building in Superior, Wisconsin. If any of you wish to go to a more definitive written account of this process, called a charrette, it has been published in the April 1991 issue of *American Libraries* by its proponent, Ted Healey, an architect from Cedar Rapids, Iowa. Simply stated, to quote Ted, " A charrette brings together librarians, library users, city officials, and architects in a planning marathon." In Superior's case, for one solid week, librarians and library staff, library users, including special interest groups, representatives from the planning groups, city officials, and various design experts from the architect's office worked almost round the clock to

complete, and gain approval, of the schematic design for the building. As Ted very wisely points out in his article, much work had been completed before the charrette began, but the process itself permitted an incredible amount of involvement by a widely disparate group of people who needed to be involved.

The process began on the first day with the various groups involved meeting together to provide input into building needs. During the evening, architects worked to design and sketch the changes and proposals that had been made. Each subsequent morning, the director, appropriate members from the library staff, the building committee, and anyone else interested in the process met with the architects to review the results of the previous day's discussion. Everyone was encouraged to be critical of the drawings and to make further recommendations for change. This went on each morning during the week until, on the last day of the week, consensus on the final drawings was achieved and the drawings were assembled into a brochure for presentation to the library board of trustees for official approval. This process served a number of useful purposes, not the least of which was the sense of ownership in the project that developed as a result of the participation of a variety of people, and particularly the library staff. Further, because of their involvement, each participant was able to, and did, speak authoritatively on the benefits of the project to the community. I recommend it to you for your consideration as you begin planning your building.

The key point in this aside is the role that library staff played in the process. True, many of them had had a hand in developing the building program statement and in making suggestions for their particular areas of involvement and responsibility. But to be able to see their advice and input put into action on a daily basis really served to boost morale and made them feel a part of the process. It really exemplified the positive role that staff can play in building a library building and underscores my feelings that it would be folly not to involve the staff in a meaningful way in your building project.

Another group of players whose involvement is important is the users. As end-users they can bring a particularly useful perspective to the design of the library building. Politically, it could be quite detrimental to the success of your project if they were not included. How they are involved remains a matter of local interest and tradition. In the academic setting in which I am most familiar, it is expected that representatives from the student body and the faculty will be involved in various capacities in the project. Representatives of user groups can be quite useful in fact finding, in designing the facility, and in helping to sell the project. End-user involvements should take advantage of various levels of expertise and influence with such appointments being made to best utilize each participant's particular talents. For example, selected friends of the library and influential alumni may be very good people to have involved, not only because they are users of the library, but for their contacts and access to power and money. How they are appointed and how they are used, however, can become a very sensitive issue and one needs to approach these appointments carefully.

As I mentioned earlier the library building consultant and the architect are two key players in the process. However, because others are discussing these two players in some detail elsewhere I won't do any more than fit them into the overall context of the building process.

The library building consultant's role may take several forms. These include, but may not be limited to, educating and guiding everyone involved through the process, assisting in the fact-finding and information-gathering process, helping to draft the library building program statement, working with the architect to see that the wishes of the library governing authority, as expressed in the program statement, are carried out in the design of the building, serving as the mediator, politician, or diplomat in settling disputes or questions, or all of the above. Typically, the library consultant will not make decisions for the governing authority but will be expected to lend expertise in seeing that the right questions are asked and answered, lines of communication remain open, and that everyone is on the same page as the project progresses. Because the library building consultant needs to be involved from the ground floor up (no pun intended) this person should be among the first appointments made by the governing authority.

Briefly stated, the architect's role is to translate the dreams and hopes of the library project team, as expressed in the library building program statement, into reality. The architect will be responsible for designing a building that incorporates form, function, and environment into a structure that will be efficient, economical, and pleasing for those who work in it and one that the client community will be proud of. When to hire the architect is a matter of discussion and the answer may depend upon local situations. However, in many cases the services of the architect are not engaged until after the program statement has been developed, agreed upon, and all systems are go.

There are a host of other players who need to be considered in the building process. Let me just briefly mention a few that you ought to keep in mind as you contemplate building a library. These include, but may not be limited to, technology experts, facilities planners, interior and exterior designers, and attorneys.

In today's fast-changing library world, one of the key areas of concern in building design is how to accommodate rapidly evolving technology. A seasoned library building consultant will be able to provide much valuable advice for accommodating technology in your building plan. However, depending upon your circumstances, you might wish to engage the services of someone who has a considerable knowledge of, and expertise in, library technology. As an example, it's fairly common to include new automated library systems in building projects, and getting advice from those who deal with such systems on a regular basis could be quite beneficial. Let me emphasize that I am not advocating that you bring in just any computer person off the street or the representative of a specific vendor, but that you consider someone who has background in library computer applications. There are a number of them out there in the library world and, while most of them do not come cheap, the return on your investment might very well be worth it. If this expertise exists in the library building consultant whose services you engage, fine and dandy. If not, you might be money ahead to seek a consultant subcontractor to assist you in this phase of the planning. Your library building consultant may be useful to you in recommending a person or firm with this expertise.

In many municipalities and on most college and university campuses you have a person or office devoted to facilities management and planning. The levels of expertise within this office may vary with the size of the institution or community but they are there for a purpose and the librarian should get to know these folks if for no other reason than keeping lines of communication open. They need to see that your project fits in with existing protocols and plans, that legal authorizations are in place, and that local customs and traditions are being adhered to. They can also serve as important sources of advice to architects, consultants, and your planning teams. In fact, it probably would not be bad to have a representative of that office serve on your committees at least in an ex officio capacity. Having such an office involved can certainly keep you from stubbing your toe as the project moves along.

The role of interior and exterior designers will more often than not be a sub-step of the architect's responsibilities. Either in the architect's firm itself or through their own resources will be a cadre of folks who will be able to provide expertise in interior design, lighting, color and signage schemes, furniture, heating, ventilating, and air conditioning (HVAC), preservation and conservation needs, parking, and landscaping, to name only a few. As you can imagine, all of these can be quite sensitive areas of discussion, and it is here that the librarian may have to exercise her or his most persuasive powers and influence. The decisions made in these areas will go a long way toward making the building a success or a failure, so one should not be shy in insuring a full and frank discussion of the proposals forwarded to address these concerns.

I hope this overview of some of the players involved in the building process is useful to you. I would reiterate, and stress, Anders Dahlgren's warning that with all of the people involved and the complexity of the process, try as hard as you may, point A may not go smoothly to point B, to C, and so on. As a librarian, though, you can be quite influential in seeing that the transition between points flows very smoothly by making sure that your levels of skills are sufficient to, if nothing else, ask the right questions. Your involvement in the selection of the balance of the project teams can be crucial, and your chances of success will increase significantly if your fellow participants possess, and represent, a broad base of abilities, expertise, and influence.

Initial Roles of the Consultant and the Planning Team

A library building project normally begins with the librarian. In by far the majority of cases, the first mention of an imminent space need comes from the head of the library, usually in his or her annual report to the library's governing authority. This is not always the case, however. Sometimes a potential donor offers to provide a new or expanded building even before anyone else has noted the need for one. In academic institutions it is sometimes the regional accrediting associations that first broach the topic, but in most cases it is the privilege and responsibility of the librarian to call attention to the need before anyone else.

This does not mean that the first mention of the need elicits a response. Indeed sometimes many, many mentions are required, each more importunate than the previous, before ultimately one day the appeal is heard, and authorization is given to initiate the planning process itself. As soon as authorization is forthcoming, a local planning committee should be appointed. Sometimes this committee can be simply an existing monitoring and or advisory group representative of the institution or service community, with its charge broadened to encompass this addi-

David Kaser is a professor at the School of Library and Information Science at Indiana University in Bloomington.

tional responsibility. More frequently, however, it is a new, ad hoc committee with the single purpose of serving as the local oversight group during the building development period.

In any event, the composition of this local committee should be broadly representative of the several constituencies in the library's service community. In a college or university, for example, it should probably comprise instructors from the sciences, humanities, and social sciences, as well as representatives from the student body and from the institution's administration. The librarian must also be a member of this group, probably serving best as its executive secretary. Later in the project, this committee will be joined by a consultant and an architect to constitute the complete planning team.

The Consultant

Indeed, as its very first task, the local committee should select a library building consultant. In medium-sized and smaller communities, especially, a consultant is essential. Such communities are unlikely to construct a library more often than once in twenty years, and as a result their local committees are unlikely to contain resident library building planning expertise. In larger institutions, moreover, where some such experience may exist locally, a consultant can still be valuable in providing an external perspective, greater acquaintance with what has been done elsewhere, and often much needed objectivity.

The selection of a consultant is facilitated by the Library Administration and Management Association (LAMA). LAMA produces a book entitled *Library Buildings Consultant List,* which gives the names and addresses, qualifications, specializations, and recent experience of individuals who have met certain minimal requirements to serve in consulting capacities. Some of these individuals are librarians, while others are architects or other design professionals. The local committee can identify several persons therein who appear to fit its needs, contact them for references and other information, and after evaluation retain the one that comes closest to what it believes it requires.

For best results the consultant should be brought into the project at the earliest possible time because he or she can save the committee much agony as well as time and money in its work. A good consultant will, first of all, help the committee understand its unique role among those of the several players who will be involved. Inputs of at least three kinds from three different sources will be necessary if the project is to succeed, and it is best if each of the three manages to keep out of the way of the other two. They are:

1. *Library Functional Input.*[1] This input comprises all of the library functional determinations that will have to be contributed to the project; providing these library functional inputs is the sole responsibility of the librarian and his or her advisors (e.g., the planning committee, the library staff, consultant, etc.).
2. *Aesthetic or Technical Input.* The provision of this kind of input is solely a responsibility of the architect and his or her advisors (e.g., engineers, design associates, etc.).
3. *Administrative and Financial Input.* Responsibility for this kind of input, including passing upon the aesthetics proposed by the architect, is solely the responsibility of the owner, usually represented by the president and his or her advisors (e.g., faculty, alumni, etc.).

It is well if each of these players is cognizant of the proprietary nature of his or her respective turfdoms

right from the start. In other words, the president should not try to dictate where in the building the reference desk should be located; that should be the librarian's prerogative to decide. Nor should the librarian try to sketch the building, because that is the inviolable responsibility of the architect.

Preliminary Decisions

The local committee, in company with the consultant, will want to examine several preliminary issues and attempt to arrive at decisions regarding them before beginning actually to plan the building. They may include, but are certainly not limited to, the five issues discussed in the ensuing paragraphs:

1. The future of the community itself should be reviewed and likely changes in it studied for their impact on the library. Population growth and demographic shifts should be projected. In academic institutions, changes in the curriculum can have major impact upon the library, as can also changes in teaching style or technique. Will remote instructional centers be added, requiring distance learning applications, or will emphasis be changed from resident to commuting student bodies?
2. Should the scope of the library's responsibilities be altered at this time? For example, should the new library building now become the site of the community's CATV (cable television) operation, or should the administration or the housing of the university's archives be merged into the library's purview for the first time? What about the institution's media services operation, which may till now have functioned apart from the library? Or the curriculum laboratory, or the language laboratory, or the study skills center, or the computer center? Is the departmental library situation likely to change in the years just ahead? Decisions on such issues such as these, which are seldom within the librarian's recognizance to make alone, must obviously be taken before the

---

1. Note that the librarian and his or her advisors are not necessarily responsible for all functional input, but only that relating to library functions per se. Library buildings often have to serve several kinds of functions—memorial, symbolic, even political—and inputs regarding these additional functions may come from a variety of sources.

library building is planned rather than afterwards, so that spatial accommodation for them can be made.

3. The likely impact of information and telecommunication technologies on the library's future must be assessed. Obviously this will impinge upon the electronic infrastructure to be installed in the new building. Perhaps an even greater issue here, however, may be how far the library anticipates that it will go in the years ahead to "bring the library to the people" instead of continuing to expect the people to come to the library. Is the library prepared to fax materials to homes, offices, or dorm rooms? Is it prepared to optically scan materials in its collection and transmit them in digitized format to patrons' personal data stores or workstations? Is it prepared to have drafts upon interlibrary services sent direct to patrons' electronic mail boxes, or indeed U.S. postal addresses? Answers to such questions as these can have great impact on the amount of in-library seating that should be planned for the new building. Also the nature and use of our neighbors' collections can have a large impact upon the amount of conventional shelf space in our own new building. Some kind of community consensus must be arrived at on some of these knotty matters before planning of the building can proceed.

4. The adequacy of the library's present organizational structure to meet the changes envisioned in the considerations above must also be appraised. Substantial population or collection growth may render the present organization chart inadequate or inappropriate. Perhaps the heads of our six functional departments have previously reported direct to the librarian, but we may soon have to have eight department heads reporting through two assistant directors. Or a new management style may call for a completely different administrative pattern. If such changes may occur, their impact upon the amount and deployment of office space throughout the new building must be determined before a building program can be drafted.

5. Also, alternatives to new construction must be considered at this point! This is not nearly as much fun as planning new buildings, but new library space costs an enormous amount of money, and as stewards of society's recorded information assets, we have an inexorable obligation to keep the cost of housing our resources and services as economical as is reasonable. Most librarians are acquainted with the strengths and weaknesses of the traditionally vaunted range of alternative spatial solutions, but we ought not to reject them at this point without looking at them one more time. Micro-reduction, compact shelving, deep weeding, and all of the others deserve one last review at this juncture so we can reassure ourselves as well as our communities that new techniques or technologies, new environmental circumstances, or new customer expectations have not provided new opportunities for resolving our space needs without going to costly new construction.

Other Involvement

Further involvements common to library building consultants will be discussed in greater detail in the next chapter. It suffices to say here, however, that additional activities in which building consultants might be involved can be myriad. After three decades of building consulting, the writer still finds himself expected on occasion to provide a completely new kind of advice or assistance. Only recently, after spending three days on a campus studying the need and prospect for a new building, the writer was asked in the exit interview with the president: "Now, my big question is 'Should I fire my librarian?'" This apparently was the president's hidden agendum for bringing an outsider to the campus at all. In this case the president did not get an answer, but she did get a scolding.

There are no lists of right and wrong things to ask a consultant to do. Again, since so few librarians have experience in planning buildings, it is very common for the client to not even know what to ask of the consultant. If that is the case, the client should simply call and say, "Help!" or inquire of the consultant what kind of help appears to be most needed. After all, one seldom goes to a physician with instructions on what he or she wants done, and although the analogy does not fit the client-consultant relationship perfectly, it has some qualities to recommend it nonetheless.

How Consultants Work

There are library-based, moonlighting consultants, and there are library consulting firms, and there are combinations of these two. Library-based consultants obviously are available only part-time, since they are under continuing salary obligation to a library somewhere. Few if any of them hang up their shingles, however, until they have worked out some kind of arrangement with their full-time employer that allows them enough scheduling flexibility so they can do justice to a consulting assignment. Most universities, for example, believe that some consulting can be both a source of growth and an outlet for service for members of their faculties, including librarians. As a result most permit (indeed some even encourage) their faculty members to consult up to say 20 percent of their time as long as their local responsibilities are fulfilled first.

Moonlighters have some advantages as consultants, and they have some disadvantages. An apparent disadvantage, of course, is that they have to schedule their availability to a client around their obligations to a primary employer. On the other hand, even very large firms have to juggle their work for one client around their work for others, so this is not a problem for free-lancers alone. Another possible disadvantage of moonlighters is that they usually work alone and can therefore bring only a single body of expertise to a job, whereas larger firms can sometimes put several different persons, each with unique competencies, on an assignment.

Moonlighters often feel that one big advantage that they bring to a consulting assignment is that they indeed are employed full-time in a library where they have to contend all day every day with library problems, so that their perceptions of such issues have more of an applied, "real-world" character than those of full-time consultants. It is probably also true in many cases that moonlighters can charge less, because in effect their consulting activities are subsidized by their primary employer. They already have a fully equipped office, for example, although most are probably cautious not to let any supernumerary expenses of their outside work fall on their home institutions. This means, of course, that their work will entail minimal overhead costs that have to be spread across their consulting fees.

This last consideration, however, should not be decisive in any event. The worst possible kind of economy in a library building project is to hire the consultant who will work for the lowest fee. The most economical consultant to retain is the one best equipped to do the job, almost without reference to his or her fee schedule.

The advantages of retaining consulting firms instead of free-lance practitioners are obviously the flip-side of the points made in the previous paragraphs. Consulting firms can sometimes move faster, they can sometimes provide a broader range of expertise, and over time they can develop more consulting experience (although usually at a compensating loss of applied library experience). They are often bonded, and they must meet state legal and incorporation requirements.

There are, of course, combinations of these two kinds. Not a few moonlighters are themselves incorporated, keep on tap ateliers of other moonlighters or indeed even full-time experts to round out their offerings, and sometimes even benefit from some subsidies from their primary employers. Whether corporations or individuals, however, most library building consultants wish that they could think of something they could call their involvement without using the term *consulting*. In the first place, the term is grossly unspecific, and partly for that reason it is viewed in many circles as one almost of social opprobrium.

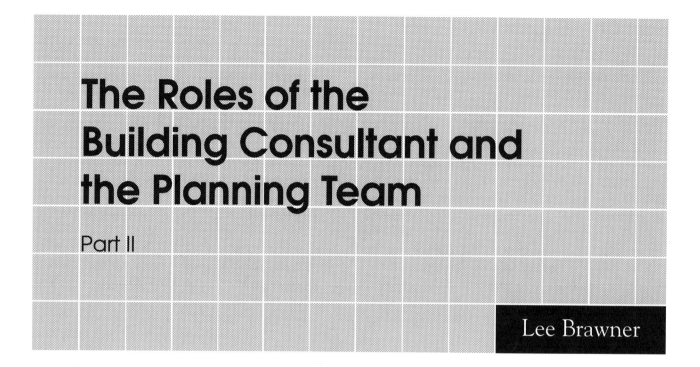

The Roles of the Building Consultant and the Planning Team

Part II

Lee Brawner

In a previous chapter David Kaser overviewed the composition, responsibilities, and roles of the planning team and the kinds of consultants available for consideration. In this companion section the following will be reviewed:

> The primary reasons for retaining library building consultants
> Typical building consulting roles
> Consulting fees, and "hidden" owner costs
> Component parts of a "generic" Request for Proposal for consulting services
> Evaluating proposals for consultation

The Building Consultant: A Library Tradition

Librarians began calling on their library colleagues to serve as building consultants as early as the 1930s. The consultations have ranged from information exchanges about solutions to building problems to formal, long-term contracts for specialized services.

Lee Brawner is the executive director of the Metropolitan Library System in Oklahoma City, Oklahoma.

Academic libraries were among the first to make extensive use of library building consultants. The post–World War II years produced a building boom for academic campuses and libraries when enrollment swelled with returning servicemen and -women. That produced an echo boom, ushering in a number of library building consultants including such luminaries as Ralph Ellsworth Mason, Keyes D. Metcalf, and others.

The building boom for public libraries came in the "golden years of the 1950s and 1960s," stimulated by the advent of the Library Services and Construction Act (LSCA) with its Title II matching construction funding. Many of these LSCA Title II programs as administered by the state libraries mandated that local libraries—without the necessary on-staff expertise—engage experienced library building consultants. That boom provided the incentive for many library building consultants, most of whom consulted on a part-time basis while holding full-time positions in libraries and library schools.

These early library building consultants provided a rich legacy, and today's consultants continue to draw on their documented experience. As libraries have evolved into more complex organizations and "smart buildings" with technologically sophisticated facilities, the role and complexity of library building consulting have changed. Today's library buildings must be planned and designed to be functional, inviting, flexible, accommodating to modern furnishings and equipment, expandable, technologically adaptive, barrier-free, energy-efficient, maintainable, aesthetically sensitive, attractive, cost-effective to operate, and constructed within budget. Co-editors Leighton and Weber, in the introduction to the second edition of Metcalf's *Planning Academic and Research Library Buildings* (ALA, 1986), address these changes and note that, "One need only look back twenty to fifty years to see the contrasts in buildings designed and constructed by different generations. Just as there are today certain conditions of aesthetic taste, financing, construction techniques, sociological expectations, and management practices, so it is predictable that in another one or two decades many of these will again change."[1]

What Constitutes an Effective Building Consultant?

There are thirty-six library building consultants listed in LAMA's 1989 *Library Buildings Consultant List*, and there are still others who did not choose to be included in the list.[2] What constitutes an effective consultant? I submit that an effective building consultant must satisfy the following qualifications:

Broad Diversified Experience

The consultant must have "been up to bat" many times in several leagues. Experience with one building project, or several building projects in one's own library system, does not meet these qualifications. An effective building consultant must have experience with a range of buildings—new buildings, renovations and additions, and conversions—of many sizes.

Current Knowledge of Building Planning or Design and Furnishings

To effectively serve the client or owner, the consultant should be expected to have a good, current working knowledge of library building planning, concepts, trends, technological needs, construction

methodologies, project costs, construction bidding and contract practices, and, of course, of library furnishings, shelving, the equipment market, manufacturers, and vendors.

Political Acumen

Most libraries and all building projects are tied in political wrappings. The effective building consultant must have the political acumen to operate effectively with the library owner in this climate. Ideally, the consultant brings experience from several other similar settings involving close communications with administrative and governing boards and bodies, public meetings, and the media. Building projects frequently place the consultant in public meetings that may be politically sensitive or confrontational in nature; the consultant must be tempered and experienced in fielding and addressing critical questions and issues in these settings.

Group Process and Interpersonal Skills

Effective building consultants work closely with the owner and the owner's representatives including the planning team; most planning processes also provide for the consultant to dialogue with advisory groups, focus groups, and user groups. In addition, the consultant will be working with the project architect, interior designer, engineers, and other special consultants in areas such as automation, acoustics, furnishings, lighting, and security systems. All of these relationships call for effective group processing and interpersonal skills.

Documentation, Writing, and Presentation Skills

A basic qualification calls for the consultant to have the demonstrated ability to document the specific needs for the building project in writing and the skills to present the report or findings in an effective format and presentation style. It is critical that the

---

1. Keyes D. Metcalf, David C. Weber, and Philip D. Leighton, *Planning Academic and Research Library Buildings*, 2nd ed. (Chicago: American Library Association, 1986), xix.

2. Jane G. Johnson, ed., *Library Buildings Consultant List* (Chicago: Buildings and Equipment Section, Library Administration & Management Association, American Library Association, 1989).

owner ascertain the consultant's skills in all of these related areas. A consultant who may be savvy in providing counsel on planning an effective building, but who can't defend the planning in a public meeting or produce a final product in the form of a building program, critical report, or other presentation, is not going to provide the services you are seeking.

Why Retain a Building Consultant?

Library administrators and governing boards are regularly called on to plan, initiate, or evaluate building projects involving new, expanded, remodeled, or reorganized buildings, or to consider the feasibility of converting an existing building to library use. Frequently, the administrators and governing boards lack the expertise on staff or the time to perform the necessary study. Or, they may elect to engage outside consultation to obtain the independent appraisal and objectivity of a third party who is removed from the library and local politics.

Building Consulting: Roles and Benefits

Before examining the typical, specific tasks and assignments that a building consultant may undertake, let me enumerate some of the general roles in which the consultant may serve as part of the consulting process. The client library can derive several benefits from these roles that will advance the consulting objectives.

Providing Knowledge and Expertise

Experienced building consultants can provide knowledge and expertise that may not otherwise be available to the library. As Rawles and Wessels state in their excellent book, *Working with Library Consultants,* "Few libraries could begin to duplicate with their full-time staff the broad array of skills which are available from consultants. . . ."[3] In effect, engaging a consultant is the equivalent of hiring a temporary specialist who can provide current knowledge and expertise beyond one's own library resources.

Providing Objectivity and Analytical Skills

The most valuable contribution a building consultant can bring to the client on a building project is objectivity—that is, objectivity based on an impartial analysis and evaluation of the client's needs and clear recommendations that are not influenced by vested interests, preconceived opinions, politics, or personal ties.

Providing Influence to Help Sell the Project

As part of the consulting contract, the owner library frequently calls on the experience and reputation of the building consultant to help sell or promote the building project to the governing body, to the public, and to the media.

Saving Time

Most library building consulting projects are directly related to the development or implementation of a long-range plan or initiation of planning for a specific building that is tied to a schedule. The building consultant helps the client library "crunch" the time to meet a demanding schedule by supplementing the library's own staff.

Assuming the Role of Educator, Facilitator, or Change Agent

As part of the process for the consultation, the library consultants regularly assume an educational role in terms of orienting staffs, boards, and related parties with basic library building planning concepts, conducting tours of other libraries, or illustrating trends and issues via slides of comparable library buildings. The consultants may also conduct focus groups and user group meetings to gain insights and reach accord on issues. Also, the consultants may function as change agents in terms of involving the staff or boards in the consideration, for example, of alternative organizational or work patterns in response to the proposed new facility.

---

3. Beverly A. Rawles and Michael B. Wessels, *Working with Library Consultants* (Hamden, Conn.: Shoe String Pr., 1984), 8.

Introducing a Creative Ferment

An effective consultant also brings to the assignment a broad cross section of experience on similar projects, a creative imagination, and perspectives for considering alternative solutions to space needs. This produces a creative ferment, as part of the consulting process, that benefits the client in terms of several approaches leading to the best solution for the particular project.

Typical Building Consulting Tasks and Assignments

So much for consulting roles and by-products of the consulting process. Let me review the most typical building consultant tasks and project assignments. In most instances, the library will directly engage the consultant for these services, although the building consultant may also be engaged directly by architects and planners to perform the services.

Space Needs Study

A space needs study usually involves one building. It includes an assessment of the current condition, determination of present and future services, space for the services, and related alternatives for same. The alternatives may include remodeling, expansion, or a new facility.

Long-range Facilities or Master Plan Study

This consultation assignment usually calls for an assessment of the total long-term, commonly twenty-year, building needs for a library or library system. The client library may provide the space planning criteria, or call on the consultant to propose same. The assignment enlarges on the space needs study described above, but broadens to address all libraries in the system. Analyzed in the context of broader community or institutional needs surveys and analysis are: the service area population or student enrollment projections; other demographic, economic, and related studies and projections; and the collection and services evaluations and organizational studies. The result is a long-range study with phased, criteria-based recommendations for location, sizing

and planning new or expanded facilities, closing facilities, and a prioritized timetable with projected cost estimates for implementing the plan.

Preparation of Written Building Program

A key, integral assignment for most consulting projects is the preparation of a detailed, written library building program or "architect's assignment" for a new building, expanded or remodeled library building, or conversion of a building to serve as a library. Researched and written in a close working relationship with the client library, the library staff, and governing board, the building program is a major planning document. It will be used to promote the project, describe the building, and serve as the formal project planning document upon approval of the governing board. It can serve as the focus document during interviews for architects and interior designers, and it will guide the building through all architectural and interior design planning phases to completion.

Consultation during Architectural Design Phases

Most library consulting contracts involve start-to-finish services. That is, in addition to the preparation of a building program, the consultant is also engaged to critique the plans and specifications for the building and the furnishings from design development phases through the final construction.

Technical

Given the technical sophistication of libraries, the building consultant may also be engaged to provide—as part of the building consulting team—specialized consultation with regard to the automation, communications, or telecommunications needs for the building project.

Site Selection

Site selection is a critical decision for any building project, especially for public libraries; it is also one of the most volatile and political decisions facing most library building projects. Building consultants are frequently engaged to evaluate prospective sites and make a recommendation for the most effective one. As the library literature and any building consultant will bear out, site selection projects can be frustrating, drawn-out assignments that tax the temperaments of all parties involved.

Selection of the Architect and Interior Designer

As part of their services contract, library consultants are often engaged to assist the library owner in the selection of the architect and interior designer for the building project. This assistance can take the form of proposing a selection process including evaluation criteria, and it may include participation as the owner's representative in the interviews. The primary role for the consultant is to help interpret the building program during this process; the owner, of course, is responsible for the final decision in selecting the architect and interior designers.

In summary, today's building consultants are called upon to serve in a variety of building assessment and planning roles, calling on their experience, expertise, and personalities. They are expected to complement their knowledge of library buildings, furnishings, space planning, and organization with skills as a teacher, researcher, and promoter. They must have knowledge of library processes and operations, technology, financing, organization, and management. Frequently, these diverse assignments involve the need for a consulting team with several specialists working together with the client to complete the assignment.

Rawles and Wessels refer to consultation as a "facilitating process" and a "partnership" where "the client brings a knowledge of his or her organization and the nature of the problems while the consultant brings problem-solving expertise and special knowledge of the area to be studied."[4]

I agree that the partnership analogy is valid. Both the consultant and the library client have distinct responsibilities in the contract, and a key to a successful project is a process that brings them together in a sharing, working relationship.

What Do Consultants Cost?

Building consultants are very flexible. You can contract for their services on a "flat" rate or so-called up-set rate for a specific building project with the understanding that the total for fees and all other related costs will not exceed a stated amount. You may engage consultants on a daily or hourly rate plus reimbursables such as travel and related direct costs. You may engage them on a percentage fee basis plus reimbursables, based on the cost of the construction and furnishings for a specific project. Depending on the scope and size or cost of the construction project, this percentage will likely range from about .5 percent to 1.5 percent. Smaller, less costly projects will generally have a higher percentage fee. The percentage basis plus reimbursables is commonly used for "start-to-finish" consultant contracts that include preparation of the building program, critique or review of all plans, and consultation through the construction phase and completion of the building.

Generally, most library consultants contract on a daily or hourly fee basis plus reimbursable expenses for travel, communications, typing or word processing, printing or reproduction, and an administrative or overhead cost percentage. The daily rate depends upon the experience and the reputation of the consultant and the speciality involved. The daily rate will vary from about $300 to $800 per day, depending on the individual consultant and the scope or degree of involvement with the project.

The library client can contain some of these costs by holding travel to a minimum, utilizing telephone conference calls in lieu of some on-site consultations, and handling the printing or reproduction of the interim and final report. In the latter instance, the library would call for only one printed copy and a reproduction-ready copy or word-processing disk copy of the reports and directly produce them locally at a lesser cost.

On the important subject of costs, the library client or owner must also consider the hidden costs inherent in the RFP process, the study, and its implementation. Consider the team members' and other staff members' time that will be spent in meetings with the consultant and in reviewing and critiquing the reports. Consider, too, the library administration staff and time needed to educate or orient the consultant to the local library and region.

Begin with an Effective RFP

The majority of library building contract agreements are awarded on the basis of consultant proposals

---

4. Ibid., 4.

written in response to owner RFPs. It behooves the owner to budget time for three important decision blocks in this process:

1. Take time to prepare a thoughtful, effective RFP.
2. Build in or allow sufficient time for prospective consultants to respond to the RFP.
3. Allow sufficient time to analyze the proposals and interview the top contenders.

A responsive proposal takes an investment of valuable time and money and deserves thoughtful consideration.

A simple, generic RFP for library building consultation calls for a qualified library consultant to prepare a building program, from consultation through all planning phases and the construction phase of the new building. The RFP sets out the time for receipt of proposals and provides a brief description of the library. It describes how the library building fits into a larger capital improvement plan and the proposed public funding for the project. The RFP requests that the proposals describing the methodology, plans, personnel, and costs be submitted for three sequential phases; the owner reserves the right to contract for one, two, or all three phases. It sets out the organization of the proposal in broad terms and calls for a statement of qualifications, examples of similar building programs or projects, proposed methodology including a timetable, the number of proposed site visits, and a detailed cost proposal for each phase. The RFP also sets out the criteria that the local committee will use in reviewing the proposals and making a selection. You will note that the RFP does not cite a budget for the consulting contract, and you may be sure that when the first prospective building consultant calls for more information he or she will be pumping

the owner for more information including the estimated budget for consulting. In most instances, I would advise the owner to state the amount budgeted for the consultation.

Regarding the evaluation of proposals, you must operate within a project budget, but I urge you not to set an arbitrary ceiling on the consulting contract. Allow the prospective consultants an opportunity to respond to your building project needs in their unique way. Weigh all of the approaches and methodologies to the project from the various consultants. Select the ones that are most appropriate to your needs and visit with those consultants; you can do this inexpensively by phone or plan the interviews around an ALA conference and meet them there as you narrow down the prospects. In an academic library setting, the consultant is occasionally brought on board as a lecturer or adjunct faculty member to provide the consultation; this is particularly appropriate if the project involves considerable group process or continuing education components. Too, the building consultant may be engaged by the project architect in consultation with the library client.

Finally, remember that the building consultants can't read your mind. When you interview them, ask about their approach and explore feasible alternatives. Settle on the consultant you believe you can work with and who can deliver the best job for your particular library and then set about to negotiate the contract. The library profession is unique in that so many outstanding librarians, recognized leaders in the field of librarianship, are also practicing consultants on both a full- and part-time basis. Tap into their expertise and compress their experience and their "times at bat" to help you hit a home run in your home stadium. They can help make your building project go smoother while minimizing staff time and producing a more functional, cost-effective building.

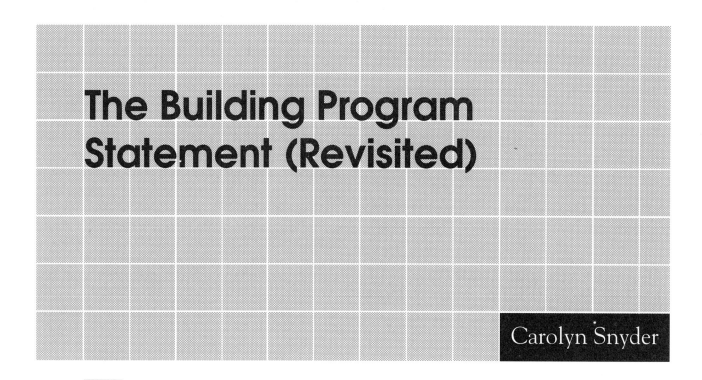

The Building Program Statement (Revisited)

Carolyn Snyder

There never was a time, I believe, when it was more difficult to design with any assurance of what was going to happen to buildings in respect to either physical, functional, or aesthetic permanence after the passage of even a few years. And yet, with the very high cost of construction and the increasing difficulty of raising capital funds for structures such as libraries, it is all the more important that we ensure in every way possible their long life and continuing utility."[1]

Although thirty-six years have passed since Robert O'Connor made his observations about the difficulties of library building planning, his words remain relevant today. As we approach another major transition for new and renovated library facilities, we face even more pronounced difficulties in predicting the future usage of libraries than O'Connor did in 1954, due in large part to rapid changes in information technology.

Technology is now an integral part of virtually every library service and operation. Business as usual—building program documents as usual—will not succeed in this environment! Through my experiences as an academic library administrator working with computing and telecommunications colleagues to plan the information technology future of my campus, I have learned that successful building programming must integrate information technology applications.

We must reexamine even the most fundamental basis of traditional building planning: the building program statement. Traditionally, the building program statement has been viewed as a written document prepared to provide the architect with detailed information about requirements for the facility. It is also generally accepted that the other purposes of the program statement are

1. a determination of facilities needs of the library by the administration and staff of the library and
2. communication with the faculty and administration about library needs and ways to deal with them.

In today's library environment, however, the building program document must also be used to communicate with companies who will design and supply telecommunications and computing capabilities for

---

Carolyn Snyder is dean of library affairs at Morris Library, Southern Illinois University at Carbondale.

1. Robert B. O'Connor, in *Planning a Library Building*, ed. Hoyt R. Galvin (Chicago: American Library Association, 1955), 30.

the library facility. A technology plan for the library, prepared by librarians in consultation with others on campus, is an essential background document for the building program process. This technology plan for the library must be prepared in the context of the technology development of the campus. For example, libraries can provide access to computerized information services in offices and dorms only if the capacity of the campus network is adequate to handle the projected increased traffic.

Another time-honored tradition in the world of library building planning is that the head librarian or senior library administrator should write the program. Indeed, such a person should chair and truly lead the building program committee, and the head librarian must have final review of the program. In today's environment, however, no one person can write a successful program for an academic library. Writing this document requires the expertise of the library automation officer and others on the library staff with technology expertise, and academic computing, telecommunications, and learning resources professionals on campus. A library's needs for information technology must be described with precision if telecommunications and computer suppliers are expected to respond with appropriate technologies.

The library administrator chairing the committee must have strong interpersonal and communication skills, since many individuals with unique perspectives must contribute to preparing and writing the program. These include library staff, users, administrators, and the institution's facilities programmer, who may assume a major responsibility for compilation of the document. The committee chair must develop a real team effort with all committee members and with the appropriate technology persons as the document is written—perhaps with different individuals preparing drafts of sections. As with most planning processes, creative thinking and careful listening are ground rules.

Consultant selections should be made with a careful assessment of the individual's current knowledge of integrating technology applications in libraries, as well as the more usual qualifications that are described in the literature. Unlike most earlier publications, Richard W. Boss' 1987 book integrates the information technology expertise in his description of the consultant's role.[2]

Obviously, institution administrators should review the final program. Beyond that, some institutions operate with facilities priority-setting committees

and faculty advisory committees. Since convincing the groups to assign a high priority to the library building project is the goal, a summary document might be useful. Campus academic computing advisory committees and campus technology planning groups are relative newcomers to the list of administrators and groups who might review library building programs.

The elements of a program document vary somewhat, but generally follow an accepted outline. See figure 1 for an example of such an outline. Variations are detailed in many items in the bibliography. I agree with the writers, especially several public librarians, who point out that service to our users must be the central focus of a building program.

The elements usually included are:

A. Description of the project
B. Need and expected contribution to educational services
   1. Description of libraries
   2. General distribution of space requirements
      Collection space needs
      User space needs
      Service space needs
      (Conversion of existing space)
C. General building considerations
D. Bubble chart of space relationships
E. Individual area descriptions
      Such as reference services and preservation department
F. Appendixes
      Such as background information, detailed charts and graphs, and the charge to the committee

In addition to these generally accepted elements of a building program, I would add a major section describing the technology plans and requirements of the library. This section could address the flexibility needed to meet future technology needs (a challenge for even the most creative technology thinkers) and the extent of remote access planned for library services, with its projected impact on on-site use.

If the planning is for an addition to a facility, integrated programming should be done for both the addition and the current facility. Most currently utilized facilities suffer from O'Connor's plight: they were not designed to accommodate the telecommunications

---

2. Richard W. Boss, *Information Technologies and Space Planning for Libraries and Information Centers* (Boston, Mass: G. K. Hall, 1987), 103, 104.

TABLE OF CONTENTS

Figure 1. Example of a Program Document

and electrical power needs of the library of today, much less the library of the future. The functional relationship of the addition and the current facility must be considered together, a concept described by David Kaser as "zero-based programs."[3]

We must remember that the building program document can and should be used to build internal and external support for the project from many agencies and individuals. At Indiana University, for example, support must come from the Office of the Vice President for Facilities, the campus administration, the central university structure, and outside agencies and individuals such as the Indiana Higher Education Commission, the state budget agency, the general assembly, and the governor. Librarians have always used the building program document to present to these decision makers the facts and justifications for the needs of the project. Today, we must also demonstrate that the library has the foresight and the ability to incorporate appropriate and creative technologies into our libraries of the future. For this reason, the building program document and process must change to integrate technologies. There is already evidence that a forward-looking building program document may be a key factor in selling major library building projects to outside funding agencies and to private funding sources.

---

3. David Kaser, "Current Issues in Building Planning," *College & Research Libraries* 50 (May 1989): 303.

Using Space Inventories, Projections, and Standards to Build a Successful Program Statement

Sonja Johnson

As program writer for Indiana University, I have worked on a dozen or more library programs and have thus become familiar with many of the problems and challenges faced by librarians today. Notwithstanding this familiarity, however, the perspective I bring to library planning is somewhat different from that of librarians. My viewpoint is that of the institution as a whole, or the owner, rather than of the building occupant or librarian. As such, I have two responsibilities to the project:

1. to verify the library's case for needing more space, and
2. to negotiate the project size and scope.

I hope to convince you of the importance of these two steps as part of the orderly planning process and to share with you some of the how-to's of achieving these two planning goals.

Making a Case for More Space

It is a rare library planning project that does not need external support of some kind. In a large, publicly funded, multicampus research university like Indiana

University, many levels of support and approval must be won before the architects can begin their work—the affected campus, the central library administration, both academic and administrative arms of the central university administration, the trustees of the university, the commission for higher education, the state budget agency, and, finally, the general assembly and governor. If there's a private component to the funding sought, the fund-raising arm of the institution and potential donors also must be convinced.

Viewed from the standpoint of potential donors, careful verification of your request makes sense because it is almost certain that you will not be the only entity seeking their support. You must provide them with the facts that will convince them that your project should be at the top of their priorities. Moreover, objective verification of need is important because libraries have an especially hard time building their case. The tough-minded critic can always find three or four inches on each shelf that still could receive books, or carrels that are not occupied 100 percent of the time.

So how can you build your case?

Take a Close Look at Existing Facilities

To assess the adequacy of current facilities, you should have floor plans and a space inventory. You also must make a physical review of your facility.

Sonja Johnson is the director of the Bureau of Facilities Programming and Utilization at Indiana University in Bloomington.

Floor Plans and Inventory

At most institutions of higher education there will be an office with a name that sounds something like "facilities programming and utilization" or "space management." By contacting that office, you should be able to get a set of floor plans of your space and a detailed inventory identifying each room by number, room-type code, function, size, station count, departmental assignment, and other characteristics.

The first act should be to make an actual physical and functional comparison of the facility to the inventory and floor plans to be sure your space is accurately reported. Make any needed corrections. You will need this information throughout the planning process as you compare existing facilities to current and future needs for the purpose of defining and justifying your request.

If you are at a small college or are in a non-higher-education setting, you may not have a facilities office to provide inventory and floor plans. In that case, you should make the investment required to have the necessary drawings made. (If you have an architectural drafting program, the students may be able to do this for you at a cost of less than $5,000.)

With drawings in hand and access to any one of a number of database programs such as Paradox or dBASE, any computer-literate staff member could, with a little training, assemble a room-by-room inventory in two to four weeks. You then are in a position to generate reports showing the amount of space dedicated to particular functions or in any room type. This database can become a powerful space management tool, capable of generating reports showing such items of information as which rooms are carpeted, which have windows, and which are stressed for stacks.

Tour Your Facility

Count the number of shelves in the different subject areas of your collection to familiarize yourself with your collection and to double-check the accuracy of your annual reporting figures.

Pick a few sections at random in each subject area and count the number of volumes each holds. Determine how many each should hold to be at working capacity. This will help you evaluate how closely your collection conforms to some of the commonly used library standards (e.g., 125 volumes per section or 0.1 square feet per volume). In addition, observe how well your shelving system accommodates oversize books.

Visit technical services and other open work areas. How much space is provided per person? Does the arrangement of workstations provide for adequate distance between neighboring video display terminals? Are cords and cables at each workstation badly tangled? And so on.

Above all, take pictures to document overcrowding and inefficiencies.

Estimating Existing Need

Apply nationally accepted planning standards adapted to your situation to estimate how much space is needed to house your current collection, existing reader stations, and existing staff areas. Compare these estimates to existing space.

Estimating Collection Needs

Base your estimate of space needs on item counts as found in your library's annual reports (provided the shelf count undertaken as part of the analysis of existing facilities indicates these reports are reasonably accurate).

Convert the number of items in each format to bound volume equivalencies. Then divide that number by the number of volumes each stack section should hold to be at working capacity to arrive at a total number of sections needed to house the colletion. Then multiply the number of sections by 10 square feet to get the total collection square-footage required. Or you can multiply the total item count by the square-footage each volume requires. In either case, the factors you use should be based on the characteristics of your collection as observed by a walk-through of your facility.

Estimating Reader Needs

To estimate reader space currently needed, count the total number of actual reader stations in the library and multiply by 25 square feet. Include stations at the card or online catalog, index tables, etc., as reader stations for this purpose.

Estimating Service Space Needs

To arrive at space needed for service points, offices, work areas, etc., determine the total number of weekly staff hours worked. Divide the total hours by hours in the full-time work week (usually forty hours). The resulting full-time equivalent (FTE) staff number should be multiplied by between 180 and

225 square feet. In general, the smaller the library, the higher the range of your multiplier, and vice-versa. This formula projects a bare-bones facility and I do not recommend it for future planning, only for this demonstration of immediate need.

If a very large proportion of your staff is part-time, you may want to divide by a number as low as, say, thirty-two hours. As a result of this change, the number of FTE staff and therefore the amount of required service space would both be increased. This increase reflects the fact that use of a large number of part-timers can lead to scheduling difficulties, with more than one person using the same space at the same time.

Comparing Existing Need to Space on Hand

Prepare a spreadsheet comparing your three estimates to the actual space on hand as revealed by your inventory. If your situation is like that of most libraries, this comparison will support not only your need for more space to support growth, but your immediate need for more space—without any growth, without improving any functional deficiencies or inefficiencies. Moreover, you have demonstrated your need by the application of nationally accepted standards to verifiable facts drawn from your specific situation, rather than by the impassioned pleas of beleaguered librarians or by a collection of citizen petitions.

Another benefit from this approach is that at a very early point in the planning process it can reveal problems that would, if left uncorrected, plague the project later. For example, by counting shelves in your existing collection area and developing a reliable estimate for the number of items per shelf, you have a tool with which you can double-check your own annual reports of collection size, an important step since it is these reports on which you will rely as you project growth into the future.

The early verification of need does some other things for your project as well. If, for example, your planning committee includes members who represent patrons and the larger community and who are not intimately familiar with the library's space need, this early presentation of the facts brings them along quickly, gives them a tool with which to represent the project to their constituencies, and prepares them for the task ahead.

This approach also highlights your areas of greatest need and could even point to some interim space shuffling that could help you through the period between planning and construction.

Estimating Project Size and Scope

Having verified the fact that you are out of space, you must estimate how much space you should have to meet future needs. It is, of course, impossible to predict with 100 percent accuracy the amount of space you will need in twenty to twenty-five years. But it is not impossible to plan well and, through careful planning, to make reasonably accurate predictions. Nor is it impossible to use the results of careful planning to achieve agreement between owner and occupant as to the size and scope of the project.

I cannot stress too much the importance of this agreement. Budgets will be built upon it; architects will design to it. The agreed-upon project size and the deliberations that have gone into making the agreement will to a great extent determine how your space needs will be met—through renovation alone, through an addition, or through entirely new construction.

Projecting Collection Size

I have used three different approaches in projecting collection growth:

1. the 4 percent-per-year compounded approach;
2. the target collection size approach; and
3. the approach that assumes average growth over the past few years can be projected safely into the future.

In today's uncertain economic times, the 4 percent-per-year approach should be used only when a library is very small or for some reason has no track record. I have used it only for very general, long-range planning purposes, and have never found it to be borne out in any of our libraries.

In projections for smaller, regional campus libraries, it may be desirable to project space need using a target collection size of 250,000 bound volume equivalencies rather than a size derived from existing numbers. This approach probably is most appropriate for long-range master planning for land-use planning purposes, and is less useful for projecting the size of an actual building.

With the third approach, you can project the space required by finding the average growth in each format over the past five years and multiplying that figure by the number of years in the planning period —a period that should be set at twenty-five years on day one of the planning process for publicly funded institutions. Adding the five years to the more normal twenty-year planning period gives a user group at least a shot at actually having twenty years' growth left on move-in day. The average should include years in which no growth or even net decrease occurred in a particular format in order to allow for future years when budget slashing or other catastrophes will occur.

Once the amount of collection growth is calculated, follow the same procedures to arrive at total collection area that you did to get the early estimate. That is, convert to bound volume equivalencies and multiply by 0.1 square feet or divide by 125 (or by whatever other number best characterizes the collection in question) to determine stack sections; then multiply stack sections by 10 square feet to calculate total collection area.

A question that must be answered, no matter which approach you choose, is how technology will affect growth. In a university setting, non-librarians frequently seem to believe that libraries no longer need growth space. Instead, it is thought that computers, high-speed data networks, online catalogs, and CD-ROMS will somehow, mystically, take care of the matter of library growth. Librarians, on the other hand, often seem to believe that the new information technologies will only add to their space need—that traditional collections will continue to grow at their normal rate and that the new information formats and the tools required to access them will be add-ons to that space.

The truth is budget driven, and falls somewhere between no growth and business-as-usual growth. Clearly, traditional collections could continue to grow at their normal rate—the stuff is out there to acquire. The same technology that theoretically should make it possible to live without paper in fact has made most of us produce more paper. But if you intend to introduce technology into your library at all, the same dollars that will buy a monograph or a serial run in paper must buy a floppy disk or a CD-ROM. For a while, therefore, the decision as to which format to buy will be very difficult.

Still, there can be no doubt that we will increasingly make the decision to buy the CD-ROM or the floppy disk and that these decisions will have the impact of diminishing the percentage of the library that collections will occupy. However, any excess collection space projected by use of this traditional method will certainly be used up by the tools readers will require to access information. Thus, any savings should be applied to reader space, which, considered by itself, would be slighted by use of traditional projection techniques.

One can argue that using this traditional method is questionable when one's goal is to build an unassailable case for more library space. However, we may not have any better tools at hand at the moment. Moreover, the traditional method, filled with uncertainty as it may be, can be sold to administrators and bureaucrats because they can relate it in a common-sensical way to what is happening in their own professional situations.

Projecting Reader Stations

Standards for the number of reader stations that should be provided for institutions of higher education do exist, but one must make a careful analysis of one's own institution in order to choose the most suitable (and consequently justifiable) standards. Variables include institutional mission and ranking and whether or not it is residential, rural, and so on. For an institution like Indiana University, an acceptable standard would be 20 percent of the full-time equivalent (FTE) enrollment for our regional campuses and 25 to 30 percent for our flagship campuses.

Before going any further, the term "full-time equivalency" should be defined. While the formula varies slightly from institution to institution, a full-time equivalent student generally is calculated by taking the total number of credit hours and dividing by 15 for undergraduate FTE and by 12 for graduate FTE. This is a very important concept much used by university administrators, reducing as it does all nuts to walnuts and allowing the comparison and study of data that would otherwise be improper to compare.

It is important, whenever enrollments are being discussed, that you know FTEs are being used. This is especially important when dealing with an institution where there are many part-time students and the ratio of FTE to head count is 50 percent or lower. Administrators of part-time, usually commuter, campuses nearly always refer to their enrollments by head count. To make this mistake in a library would be like planning the same amount of space for a single microfiche as one would for a single bound volume. There are challenges involved in planning for either, but the end result should be quite different.

Other factors enter into this calculation of how many reader study stations should be provided. Is the library facility under consideration the only library in the institution, or is it supplemented by branch libraries in other departments? Is the campus it serves in one location, or is it divided between two or more sites?

Once you have determined the total number of library seats that should be available on a campus, all library seating on that campus has to be taken into account when determining how many seats should be in any specific library. Therefore, the 300 seats that are in the music library must be subtracted from the 7,000 total seats that should be available on the campus, and so on. Furthermore, given that a student can sit only in one place at one time, all patron stations in the library, even those that are probably more accurately called "patron service stations," must be included in the count.

But even so, there are gray areas. What about a bibliographic instruction room? Certainly library patrons are seated there (and consequently cannot also be seated elsewhere) and certainly it is within the library. Still, it is probably best not to include this seating as part of the total "seating available in libraries" for your campus. That's because it really cannot be used for study or collection access on any basis but a structured one, and consequently is outside the intent of the formula.

What about an online catalog cluster or even individual terminal that is not in a library? Should this seating be considered to meet part of the total need? In general, such remote stations should not be counted as meeting part of the library requirement—except to reassure librarians nervous about the amount of seating the formula generates for their facility.

In truth, the remote use of the library will become a significant factor during the lifetime of libraries being programmed and built today. It will also become more and more difficult to solve library space problems with new buildings. Suitable sites will become harder to find and often will be prohibitively expensive; the costs of construction, operation, and maintenance of new space will become more and more difficult for public institutions to accept. The standards we use to project library space need will have to change if we are to cope with these pressures.

Having decided how many patron stations you can justify in your library, you must project how much total space they will occupy. Again, it is advisable to figure on using 25 square feet per station. A larger station size could be used to project the amount of space required to accommodate the tools of information access that will be used at many reader seats. Remember, though, that the larger amount of reader space needed can be captured from the savings that will mount up as library collections become dominated by information in electronic or other micro formats.

Projecting Service Space Need

Most guides to library planning suggest that between 20 and 25 percent of the total of reader and collection space is needed for service. In general, larger libraries are lower in the range and smaller libraries are closer to the top. However, because this number is so dependent upon the number of staff employed by the library, it is one that is likely to be scrutinized by whatever entity meets the payroll.

To prepare for this scrutiny, you may want to make the service number as small as possible. Seek out hard information about the level of budget commitment for staff your dean, or president, or director, will make to you during the planning period. Plan specifically for that number of staff using the same formula you used to determine existing space need (180–225 assignable square feet for each FTE staff member).

If you cannot get hard information, look at the relationship of staff to collection maintained during a representative period in the past and project a similar relationship into the future. This frugal approach will reduce your service space need. In a small library, however, use of this formula is almost sure to project too little space for service.

Another way of preparing for the scrutiny of payroll entities entails the justification of a number that may seem too large to outsiders. Remind them of the impact of technology on the space required for processing library materials. Tell them that the technology-rich technical services areas are the ones that tend to come up shy most often—a problem attributable to the equipment itself.

The equipment problem is complicated by the fact that we are currently at a transitional stage in our use of technology, working with both traditional and advanced technologies side by side. It is also complicated by our use of insufficiently compatible technologies, which doubles and even triples the equipment load at stations being projected and programmed according to more streamlined standards.

Finally, remind those who might question the amount of service space in your projection that it includes not only staff work spaces but also service points, lockers and lounges, mail rooms, receiving rooms, and storage areas.

Comparing Projected Need to Space on Hand

By this point in the early planning process, you will have accumulated a great deal of information. You know what space is available to you now, what your current deficiencies are, and what you will require at the end of the twenty-five-year planning period.

Add your projected need to the spreadsheet used to compare existing space to current need. You now have, in a single, simple report, all the information you need to develop a firm estimate of project size, and to decide the project scope. Will it entail an addition only? Are addition and renovation required? Or will you require a completely new structure?

You also have a realistic planning tool that demonstrates your complete understanding of your needs, which can then be used as the basis for your bid to win the institutional or governmental approval you must have for a successful project.

On the following pages are examples of all the tools I have discussed—a sample floor plan (figs. 1–3), a sample inventory (table 1), and a spreadsheet comparing existing space, existing need, a twenty-five-year projection of need, and actual program for one of the Indiana University system libraries (table 2).

Also included are the formulas I used to reach bound volume equivalencies (fig. 4). It should be pointed out that converting to bound volume equivalencies is only one way of understanding space needed for library collections. What recommends this method over others is the end product, which is a single number, and the fact that its use in other formulas is very simple. However, it is not applicable during programming, at which time you need specific information about the space requirements of each format.

Conclusion

Last, consider the following additional steps the programming committee can take, using the tools already discussed, to build external approval for the project.

Once the program is complete, make a reality check. Assemble the programmed space into collection, patron, and service categories. Compare each to your projection.

If you've done a good job, the projection and program totals will be very similar. If they vary widely, say by more than 5–7 percent, take a second look at your work. If you've used a spreadsheet for your projection and have checked data entry carefully, the projection should be the more objective document. So take a close look at the program. If you cannot identify and either justify or substantially reduce the differences between program and projection, reexamine the projection.

Once you are reassured that your program is a success from the point of view of being justifiable and thus supportable, you must do several things to assure that it will be a success when translated into design.

On any campus certain critical units should review a program statement before it is submitted to an architect. Relevant entities for a library include the physical plant, environmental health and safety, university computing services, communications services, disabled student services, audiovisual services, housekeeping, and possibly others.

These reviews typically generate changes that must be integrated into the program. Sometimes these changes are so extensive or hold so much potential for physical implications in the library that the programming committee must reconvene to review and evaluate them.

Winning and maintaining administrative and bureaucratic support for the project as it develops also must be undertaken. This entails the following:

Facilities people must be kept well-informed of the project's status.

If the project is a branch or regional campus library, the central library administration must be kept informed and given the opportunity to review and have input to the program.

Campus and university administration and the university governing body must be given appropriate opportunities for review, comment, and input.

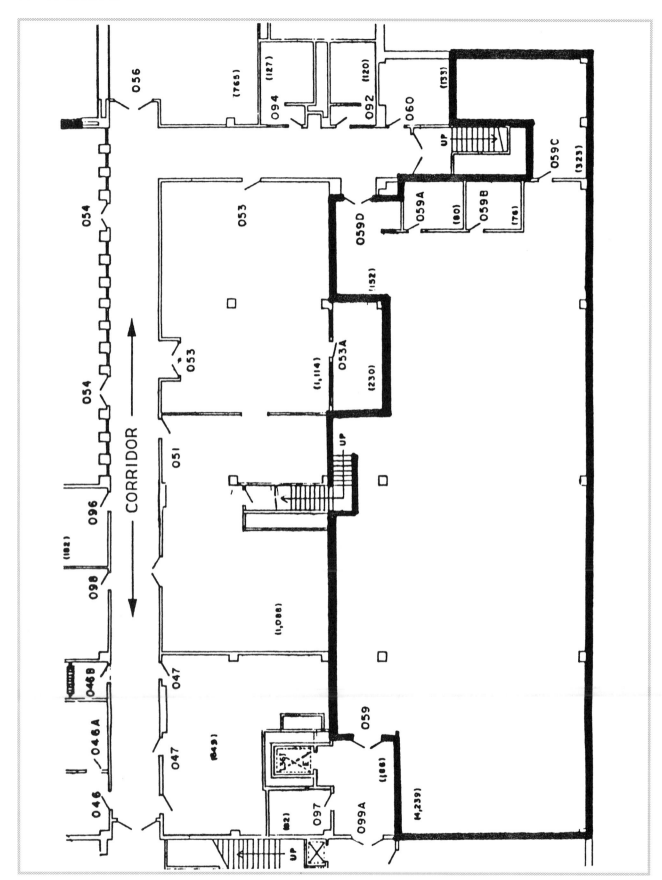

Figure 1. First Level, IU Kokomo Library, Indiana University, Kokomo, Indiana

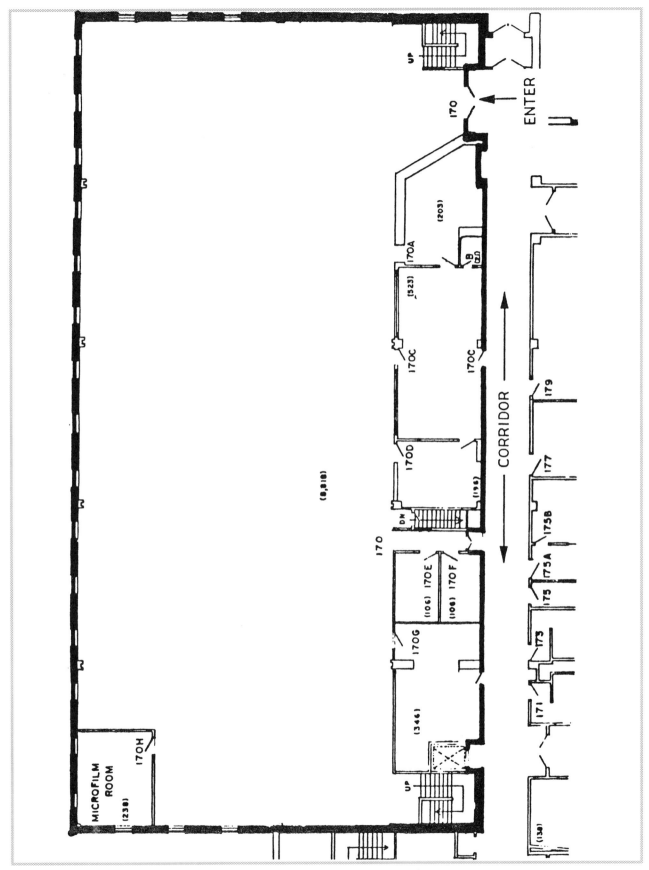

Figure 2. Second Level, IU Kokomo Library, Indiana University, Kokomo, Indiana

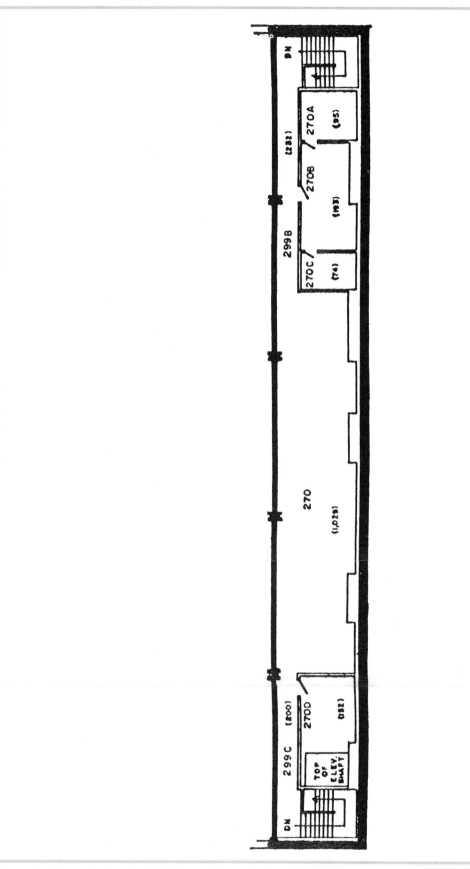

Figure 3. Mezzanine Level, IU Kokomo Library, Indiana University, Kokomo, Indiana

Table 1. Indiana University Space Inventory by Department in Building Order for Fall 1990

Department Name: LIBRARY

Building Number	Building Name	Level	Room Number	Stations	Room Type	Room Type Description	Net Area	Prorated Area	Proration Number	Room Description
860	Kokomo Main	01	059	0	420	LIBR STACKS	4,239	4,239	1	Stacks
		01	059A	2	410B	STUDY ROOM	80	80	1	Tutoring
		01	059B	2	410B	STUDY ROOM	76	76	1	Tutoring
		01	059C	8	410B	STUDY ROOM	323	323	1	Study
		01	059D	0	440	LIBR STACKS	152	152	1	Children's Lit.
		02	170	100	410A	LIBR READING	8,818	2,205	1	Reading
		02	170	0	420	LIBR STACKS	8,818	6,084	2	Stacks
		02	170	47	410C	CARRELS	8,818	529	3	Carrels
		02	170A	2	440	LIBR SERV	203	203	1	Circ. Desk
		02	170B	0	315	OFC SERVICE	21	21	1	Rest Room
		02	170C	3	310G	OFC CLERICAL	523	523	1	Work Room
		02	170D	1	310E	ADMIN OFC	196	196	1	Director
		02	170E	1	310D	ACAD/PROFES	106	106	1	Librarian
		02	170F	1	310D	ACAD/PROFES	106	106	1	Librarian
		02	170G	4	530	RADIO/TV ST	346	346	1	AV Wkshop/Study
		02	170H	1	440	LIBR SERV	238	238	1	Microfilm
		03	270	0	420	LIBR STACKS	1,029	689	1	Stacks
		03	270	0	440	LIBR SERV	1,029	340	2	Circ. Space
		03	270A	0	440	LIBR SERV	95	95	1	Graphics-Print
		03	270B	0	440	LIBR SERV	193	193	1	Graphics-Shop
		03	270C	0	440	LIBR SERV	74	74	1	Graphics-Darkrm
		03	270D	0	420	LIBR STACKS	152	152	1	Stacks
		03	299B	0	440	LIBR SERV	232	232	1	Corridor
		03	299C	0	440	LIBR SERV	200	200	1	Corridor
Total				172				17,402		

Table 2. Spreadsheet Comparing Existing Space, Existing Need, Future Need, and Program Space for the Indiana University Kokomo Library

Type of Space	Existing Space (asf)	Existing Need (asf)	Future Need (asf)	Actual Program (asf)
Collection	11316	12500[a]	22250[d]	207880[h]
Study	3213	10000[b]	10500[e]	13210[i]
Service	2873	2700[c]	8200[f]	8745[j]
Total	17402	25200	40950[g]	42735[k]

[a] 124,897 bound volume equivalencies $\times$ .1 SF per volume.

[b] 20 percent of 1986 FTE students $\times$ 25 asf.

[c] 12 FTE staff $\times$ 225 asf.

[d] 3000 volumes a year growth in books and bound volumes and a doubling of the rest of the collection.

[e] 20 percent of 2100 FTE students $\times$ 25 asf.

[f] 25 percent of reader and collection space.

[g] This number, taken into consideration with existing space, will help you decide scope of project; most critical question is whether site is large enough for addition of 23,548 assignable square feet (the difference between need and existing).

[h] As suggested, collection size is less in program than in projection.

[i] Reader space is greater in program than projection.

[j] This number exceeds program chiefly because the library houses some functions that typically are not generated by projection formulas (an AV department, a Graphics department).

[k] The program is 4.4 percent larger than the projection.

BOUND VOLUME EQUIVALENCIES

All conversion factors have been tested for the appropriateness of their application to Indiana University collections. Where the selected factor differs from the Bareither model, an explanation is provided. An explanation also is given when the type of material requires additional definition.

TYPE OF MATERIAL	CONVERSION RATIO UNIT TO VOLUME
Roughly Classified Pamphlets	15.00 to 1
Included in this category are printed materials, manuscripts, and photos	
Microfilm Reels	4.00 to 1
Microfiche	250.00 to 1
Bareither conversion factor treats only micro*film;* this factor based on observation	
Slides	200.00 to 1
Bareither has no conversion factor for slides. Use of 200 to 1 assumes a rough equivalency between fiche and slides	
Sound Recordings	6.00 to 1
Visual Materials	1.50 to 1
Category includes videotapes, film reels, film strips; factor chosen is based on observation	
Realia and Mixed Media	.67 to 1
Category includes mostly materials in boxes, kits; conversion factor chosen is based on observation	
Maps and Charts	9.00 to 1
Scores	2.50 to 1
Bareither conversion ratio of 15 to 1 changed as a result of actual observation of Indiana University collection	

Figure 4. Formula Used to Determine Bound Volume Equivalencies

Source: Adapted from conversion factors found in Harlan Bareither and Jerry L. Shillinger, *University Space Planning: Translating the Educational Program of a University into Physical Facility Requirements* (Urbana: Univ. of Illinois Pr., 1968).

In a publicly funded institution, you will, in addition, have to gain the approval of a variety of outsiders in order to move the project along. In the case of Indiana University it is the higher education commission, state budget agency, general assembly, and governor. Direct interaction of the programming committee with any of these bodies is relatively rare, but if the committee does its homework, others will have the facts and justifications to present on the project's behalf.

In these remarks, I have focused chiefly on the use of a variety of planning tools and techniques to verify the library's case for more space and to arrive at an agreed-upon size and scope for the project. I hope that I have been able to persuade you that even though these steps are taken very, very early in the planning process, they are critically important in achieving adequate funding for the project and good building design.

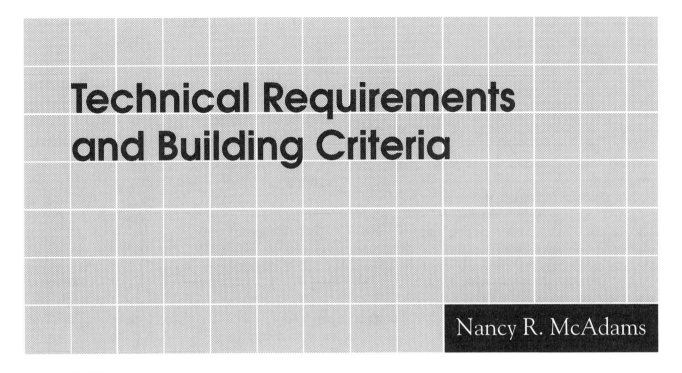

Technical Requirements and Building Criteria

Nancy R. McAdams

The process of creating an architectural design for a library building is a complicated one. It is made more complicated by the need to provide for a number of very practical conditions that we can call technical requirements of the building. Among others, they include:

    environmental control
    light, power, and communications
    fire and life safety
    security of people and property
    strength
    durability
    vertical movement
    handicapped access

The library building programmer will want to address these technical requirements for the building in the program document, defining at the very least the minimal criteria for each category of need. However, the programmer must proceed cautiously, following careful research, so that the program criteria are realistic, achievable, and non-contradictory. The program document must not require the design team to achieve the impossible.

The means for meeting the technical conditions of any building to be used by the public are determined in large part by codes, standards, and guidelines that have been developed over time by many jurisdictions: national, state, and local. Codes are derived largely from the body of law dealing with the police powers of the state, i.e., the protection of the public from harm. The formulation of these governmental regulations has been greatly influenced and augmented by consensus codes and standards established by national associations of building officials, fire professionals, insurers, and others concerned with the health and safety of the public.[1] Many state and local regulatory codes adopt or amend the national consensus codes, so that they do in fact become law.

Library planners and managers need to understand those conditions that are governed by regulatory controls, so that they can be properly addressed not only in programming, design, and construction, but also in the operation of new and existing library

Nancy R. McAdams is president of McAdams Planning Consultants, Inc., in Austin, Texas.

1. Foremost among these are the *Uniform Building Code*, issued by the International Conference of Building Officials (Whittier, California), and the *Life Safety Code*, issued by the National Fire Protection Association (Quincy, Massachusetts). Both are updated and revised frequently, and each has been adopted whole or in part by many governmental jurisdictions as the basis for local codes.

facilities. Of paramount importance is an understanding of the *Life Safety Code*. The overarching concept of "life safety" is a major determinant in building design—in architectural planning for the shapes of spaces, the placement of stairs and openings, and the characteristics of the building envelope; and in engineering design for protective construction, fire detection and suppression systems, air handling systems, backup lighting and power systems, and the like.

It is the responsibility of the architect to identify the governing codes for a given project, to design the building in accordance with code requirements, and to ensure that the constructed building is in compliance with the codes. It is the responsibility of the library planner, as client and manager, to acknowledge the many constraints on facility design and space use that are imposed by code requirements, and to maintain code compliance in the occupied building.

Building Criteria

The kinds of building conditions for which criteria may need to be established in the program document can be grouped broadly into

1. architectural design guidelines,
2. engineering design criteria,
3. security requirements,
4. handicapped access requirements,
5. building maintenance considerations, and
6. criteria for library-specific equipment and furnishings.

While it is convenient to discuss them neatly grouped into categories, in reality there are many linkages and interrelationships between them.

Architectural Design Guidelines

External and internal matters of design that can be considered in this category include, for example, the relationship of the proposed building to its site and neighborhood, the prevailing scale and texture of the environs, the architectural character or ambience to be attained, or materials to be featured or avoided. If the project concerns a historic structure or landmark site, the program document should comment on its significance as well as on any constraints arising from the historic status of the property. If the project is located on an academic campus

or within a community that has established urban design, landscape or architectural design guidelines, or has extraordinary land-use restrictions, these should be referenced in the program document.

Engineering Design Criteria

Included in this category are structural, mechanical and electrical design requirements, the issues of daylighting and acoustics, and the requirements for vertical transportation of people and materials. The program should focus on the anticipated performance of the building; i.e., what the building should do to function as a library.

The structural criteria to be established in the program document are those which are specific to libraries; i.e., floor loading appropriate to book storage, and a structural module which permits efficient bookstack arrangements. Regular library bookstack loading is generally defined in the national building codes as a design live-load of 125 or 150 pounds per square foot; if greater load-bearing capacity is needed for more intensive storage methods, the program should define the higher live-load requirement. If the program document specifies a structural bay size based on the spacing of bookstack ranges, the programmer should make certain that the resulting range aisle widths are compatible with the clearance requirements for handicapped access. For projects in locales subject to seismic hazards, the program should point out the need for floor anchoring of bookstacks so that the design of structural floors may take this condition into account.

The mechanical criteria for the building are those which establish the operating characteristics of climate control equipment: ambient temperature ranges, relative humidity ranges, air change and filtration requirements. These should be defined for the general conditions of human comfort, as well as for areas requiring preservation conditions for library materials, and for special circumstances such as computer rooms, photographic labs, food service kitchens, or indoor parking. The program document should inform the design team of any local systems for energy management by which the building will be controlled, as well as local energy conservation restrictions to which it will be subject. Other mechanical criteria which may need to be addressed are special considerations for the placement of plumbing fixtures or the routing of building piping, roof drains, site irrigation piping, or fire sprinkler systems, to avoid water damage to library materials or equipment.

The electrical criteria for the building involve the requirements for interior and exterior lighting (illumination levels, fixture types, controls) and for power distribution and backup, as well as the requirements for voice and data communication, for security and fire protection alarms, for electronic locks and clocks, and for media distribution or public address systems. Again, these should be described in terms of performance: what the systems should do. The emphasis in the program document should be on

1. conditions peculiar to library usage,
2. those conditions subject to change over time, and
3. energy management or monitoring relationships between this building and related buildings.

A program statement on daylighting should indicate whether natural illumination is desired, relative to the need to protect library materials from the harmful effects of sunlight. A descriptive statement on acoustics should describe the kind of acoustical environment expected, identify the potential sources of intrusive sounds (street traffic, telephones, copiers, etc.), and identify areas of the building requiring full acoustical separation (meeting rooms, restrooms, etc.). Finally, a discussion of vertical transportation should explain the anticipated needs for movement of staff, the public, library materials, and other service loads so that the designers can determine the appropriate locations, and the types and sizes of escalators, elevators, conveyors or lifts.

Security Requirements

Library security concerns the protection of property and the protection of people, and derives from a combination of design, equipment, and operational policy. The building program document should inform the designers of the specific measures to be taken in the facility. These might include entrances and exits controlled by guards, hardware, or alarms; separate zones of access for the public, staff, and maintenance personnel; electronic surveillance of sensitive areas; locked or sealed windows; lines of sight for observation of public spaces; interior and exterior lighting; and communication devices. The design objective should be to establish an environment which supports personal safety and minimizes the potential for property damage or loss, within manageable limits.

Handicapped Access

Since libraries are, by and large, public facilities, they are required by law to be accessible to persons with impaired mobility, sight, or hearing. The program document need not address the access modifications for such usual building features as stairs, elevator controls, drinking fountains, restrooms, etc., but it should point out those conditions which are peculiar to libraries: access to bookstacks, card catalogs, copy machines, computer terminals, media equipment, study carrels, and the like; accommodation at service desks; and configurations for staff areas which allow for the employment of handicapped persons.[2]

Building Maintenance Criteria

Libraries typically do not expect to be able to refurbish buildings or replace furnishings as often as commercial building owners do, even though the public sometimes subjects libraries to hard use. The designers should be made aware of the need for durability and ease of maintenance in the selection of building materials and finishes. The building program should delineate the anticipated hours of service to the public, the expected level and frequency of janitorial services, and the provisions to be made in the design for storing janitorial supplies and equipment, for trash collection within the building, and for the accumulation and removal of garbage and recyclable materials.

Criteria for the Selection of Collection Storage Equipment

The program document should provide specific information about the kinds of library shelving, cabinets, and specialized furnishings to be used for the containment of library collections. The programmer

---

2. The most significant national regulations governing handicapped access are ANSI Standard A117.1 (American National Standards Institute); the *Uniform Federal Accessibility Standards,* issued jointly by the General Services Administration, the Department of Defense, the Department of Housing and Urban Development, and the U.S. Postal Service (FED-STD-795, revised 1988); and the proposed rules developed by the Architectural and Transportation Barriers Compliance Board (36 CFR Part 1191) relative to the Americans with Disabilities Act (ADA) of 1990. Some states and municipalities have established their own access requirements; some of these vary significantly from the national regulations. Standards similar to those in the U.S. have been established in the *1985 National Building Code of Canada.*

should not assume that design personnel will be sufficiently familiar with this kind of equipment to be able to determine its capacity or to design effective layouts, much less to prepare specifications for its purchase and installation. Library shelving should be described according to its type, material, finishes, dimensions, spacing, bracing, and anchoring (including provisions for seismic hazards). High-density shelving systems should be defined as to type, materials, dimensions, operating characteristics, power and structural requirements, and floor treatment. Storage cabinets for microforms, maps, or media should similarly be defined as to material, finishes, dimensions, drawer configurations, and anticipated weights when loaded. The designer should be advised of the need to develop the details of service desks and other functional furnishings collaboratively with library personnel.

Conclusion

The building program serves as a kind of recipe or road map for the architectural and engineering design professionals as they proceed with the many interlocking details of planning the library building. It is the programmer's task to see that the members of the design team understand and appreciate the ways in which library buildings, in general, differ from other building types and the ways in which this library, in particular, chooses to operate. The program document should focus on these differences, delineating them in technical terms whenever possible, so that the finished building can provide the conditions necessary to meet this library's specialized needs.

Functional Requirements and Space Relationships

William W. Sannwald

This chapter deals with the functional requirements and space relationships that must be considered in planning new library buildings, and covers the time period from when the library committee has finished its written program until the architect presents the first schematic drawings to the library. This is the time when the architect or designer works with the library staff and programmers to determine the basic functions within the building, and translates the written building program into space relationships. It is likely that a program will have been prepared either by the library staff, institutional staff, or by a building consultant, but not by the architect, although sometimes the architect is brought into the process early on and does play a significant role in programming.

This time period is a cycle of continuous communications between the library building team, the architect, and other interested persons. In the case of a university, interested persons might include the administration, faculty, and students, while in a public library, examples might include elected officials, community groups, and government administrations.

What occurs in this cycle is taking the written space projections found in the building program, and transforming words into a physical form that may be reviewed by the client. The end product is a physical representation of what will be taking place in the proposed library building, but not a floor plan. The representations arising from these activities will show relationships between the various sections and departments within the library.

In addition to describing some of the communication and adjacency techniques that will occur during this period, I will illustrate the process by using a model for a 35,000-square-foot regional library in Chula Vista, California. This exercise concentrates on interior functions by employing bubble diagram studies that occur when converting a program into library space.

The Library Program

In order to understand functional and space relationships, it is necessary to understand the role of the building program. The library's program will involve specific information about its requirements which the architect needs in order to design the facility. Programming is an information processing technique of identifying and defining the design needs of a

---

William W. Sannwald is the director of the San Diego (California) Public Library.

facility and communicating the requirements of the client to the designer. It includes not only the expressed needs of the client, but all of the human, physical, and external factors which will influence the design.[1]

There has been controversy over whether programming is the exclusive responsibility of the client, an area in which the architect should assist only, or a task in which the architect should play a leading role. As indicated above, this chapter assumes that the architect does not take part in programming. However, most architects agree that programming is clearly within the scope of design, whether it is viewed as a separate service or an indistinguishable part of the design process; or whether the program is provided by the library staff, the designer or architect, or by a third party such as a facilities space planner.

A program is the client's statement of design requirements, and the designer's instrument for meeting those requirements. In the process of examining functional requirements and space relationships, the program is used by the client in deciding the feasibility of a project, determining if facility needs have been adequately addressed, and for making project and budget authorization decisions. The program is used by the designer as a guide to the design criteria which must be fulfilled, as a source of data for preparing design solutions, and as a reference for making and evaluating design decisions.

What Drives Design?

A number of factors drive design in the building, and must be understood by both the architect and library staff in order to determine their influence on function and arrangement of the building.[2]

User needs should probably be given the highest priority. Some issues to consider include who will be using the library, and what are their motives for using the building? What are the demographic characteristics of users and what types of interactions will be taking place in the building? What are user preferences for privacy, comfort, security, access, and control, and what type of user behaviors and customs determine how the library building will be used? What types of interactions will take place within the space, including communications, relationships, transfer of materials, etc.? Staff needs are of prime importance. The staff is concerned with most of the same issues as the users, but may look at things from

a different point of view. For example, users may want reading spaces that afford maximum privacy while staff may want to supervise user activities more closely. Users may want unrestricted access to all library materials while staff may want to control the distribution of some items. Needs and wants may need to be negotiated to satisfy conflicting requirements of both users and staff.

The activities taking place inside the building must also be examined. What library services are the most popular, how should they relate to one another in space, and how do they relate to their satellite departments? Are any of these services or departments expected to expand at a quicker rate than others, and are any expected to be phased out over the next few years or substantially reduced in size?[3]

Security needs for users, staff, books, and media need to be considered. Staff and users should feel safe and comfortable both inside the building as well as in the areas adjacent to the library. The environment for books and materials should protect and extend the life of printed materials and media.

Other issues may influence the building's design and arrangements. Factors such as legal and land use restrictions, climate, site conditions, building codes, space, and energy factors may require modifications to some of the needs expressed in the library's program. For example, consider a library site that is divided in two by an access drive that cannot be moved because of zoning requirements and utility easements. This of course influences the shape and design of the building.

All of these issues must be examined during this phase because their answers influence functional relationships.

The Functional System

Apart from the physical entity of the building there is another activity taking place at a separate level within the building that must be considered before design begins. This is the functional system or opera-

---

1. Mickey A. Palmer, *The Architect's Guide to Facility Planning* (Washington, D.C.: American Institute of Architects, 1981), 287.

2. Wally Gordon, "Gaming Techniques Used in Developing Schematic Design" (San Diego: Deems, Lewis, McKinley, 1991).

3. Aaron Cohen and Elaine Cohen, *Designing and Space Planning for Libraries: A Behavioral Guide* (New York: R. R. Bowker, 1979), 250.

tional system that consists of activities and relationships that are organized for the accomplishment of the library's specific role, that is, structured to accomplish the mission of the library. The only reason for the construction of a library building is to facilitate the existence and performance of the mission or functions of the library. The functional system is comprised of separate, but frequently overlapping functions that can be classified into three categories: primary, secondary, and support functions.[4] Primary functions are those related to achievement of the organization's objectives. For a library, a primary function is housing of books and other collections in a variety of accommodations for ease of access.[5]

Secondary functions are those related to the support, maintenance, or performance of individual primary functions. Secondary function examples are the loaning of items from the book and media collection and the use of the collections to answer user questions. The latter secondary function may also support another primary function of the library—the provision of information or reference services.

Support functions are those designed to support and maintain the functional system. These include operations generally common to different types of facilities such as communications, lighting, comfort conditioning, circulation, mechanical and electrical service, and waste disposal.

Through the analysis of functional or activity systems, the designer can create a model or nonphysical infrastructure on which to base the analysis and recommendations pertaining to physical needs. Such analysis consists of:

1. Identifying functional or activity components.
   What will actually be taking place in the library space?
2. Assessing relevant dimensions or attributes of individual components.
   How much space is needed and what special activities will take place in the space?
3. Rating or ranking components according to relative significance and organizational status.
   What are primary, secondary, and support activities?
4. Identifying relationships among components.
   Do these activities need to work together, or can they stand alone?
5. Grouping components according to interdependencies.

What individual functions need to be brought together in logical blocks of functions?
6. Establishing performance goals, requirements, or criteria.
   What is expected and needed for each component?
7. Resolving conflicts among components.
   Maybe all public service departments want to be on the first floor in a five-story building. Resolution of this conflict will take both analysis of functions as well as diplomacy in dealing with section heads.
8. Organizing or reorganizing components into an efficient, effective system.
   This is the reason that this time period is one of constant communications. All members of the building team have to work together to come up with the best possible solutions.[6]

One important element to remember when analyzing spatial relationships is that the relationships between spaces are not necessarily reciprocal. The manager of technical services, for example, might want to maintain visual contact at will with the process that books take from the time they are received until they are ready to go out the door and onto the library shelves. However, the manager may not want all of the people involved in the process to have contact with him.[7]

The Importance of Communication

Converting the functional system described in the building program into design requires extensive communications between all members of the library building team.[8]

The owners of the building are defined as the people representing the organization that will occupy the new library. Their needs and wants, expressed

---

4. Palmer, *The Architect's Guide to Facility Planning*, 94–98.

5. Keyes D. Metcalf, Philip D. Leighton, and David C. Weber, *Planning Academic and Research Library Buildings*, 2nd ed. (Chicago: American Library Association, 1986), 1.

6. Palmer, *The Architect's Guide to Facility Planning*, 94–95.

7. Manuel Marti, Jr., *Space Operational Analysis: A Systematic Approach to Spatial Analysis and Programming* (Mesa, Ariz.: PDA Publishers, 1981), 214.

8. Metcalf, Leighton, and Weber, *Planning Academic and Research Library Buildings*, 56–89.

through a library committee, must be communicated to the designer during this stage. Users, such as students and community leaders, should have input into the design process to make sure that their needs are met. In our public library situation, community groups play a key role in the design process. We solicit program and design comments from community groups before we begin programming, and revisit the community planning groups at least three times before the building is sent out to bid.

Programmers must communicate with the designers to clarify functional issues and needs described in the building program. Consultants, if they are used, should take part in order to ensure that the design process is not compromising the essential nature of the library program. Consultants and programmers, because of their training and experience, help the design process flow smoothly during this stage.

The architect-designer plays the key role in coordinating the conversion of a verbal program into a functional design. The library building team presents the architect with the functional problems and requirements, and the architect studies them and solves them. Designers must interpret both the spoken as well as unspoken needs of their clients, understand the many constraints inherent to the project, and be sensitive to all groups who have an interest and a stake in the library building. All of this takes place while the designers are trying to devise a building that is functional as well as aesthetic within a budget. Architects have a tough job! One very important step to remember is all meetings and conversations that take place during this period should be recorded and reported to all who are taking part in the design process.

Techniques Used to Illustrate Functional Relationships

There are a number of methods that may be used to illustrate functional relationships within the library. Some of the most commonly used practices include the following: Social maps (fig. 1) are a useful and interesting technique that helps in laying out administrative and work areas in a library. They may be used both in new projects as well as in reorganization and remodeling. In this procedure, people who work in a space are asked which single individual they prefer to work with most closely. The individual social preferences are

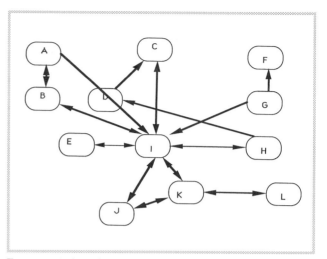

Figure 1. A Social Map

plotted on a layout diagram which shows an individual's perceived needs for contact. Preference is indicated by a directional line leading from one individual's position and pointing to the preferred individual's position. Results give information on how best to physically organize an office for easy interaction. The technique is useful for showing how to arrange an office area for relational preferences, either in terms of the functional organization or physical setting, and for identifying and defining the underlying social structure of a formal organization.[9]

One of the most commonly used devices for identifying, defining, or measuring the relationships among individual items of information in a program is a functional relationships matrix. A matrix or grid is a relatively simple device that, in its basic form, consists of vertical columns intersecting horizontal rows. We all use this type of matrix device when we consult a bus schedule or a road map.[10]

The kinds of information which may be processed by a matrix that are helpful in this stage of the library design process include functional relationships, organizational relationships, space relationships such as adjacency and proximity, activity relationships, preference measures, and priority ranking of relationships.

As an example of this technique, functional relationships for the science library at the University of California–Irvine (UCI) list forty-nine separate functional areas in Public Services, Technical Services, and Common Areas (fig. 2). The results of the

9. Marti, *Space Operational Analysis*, 102–7.
10. Ibid.

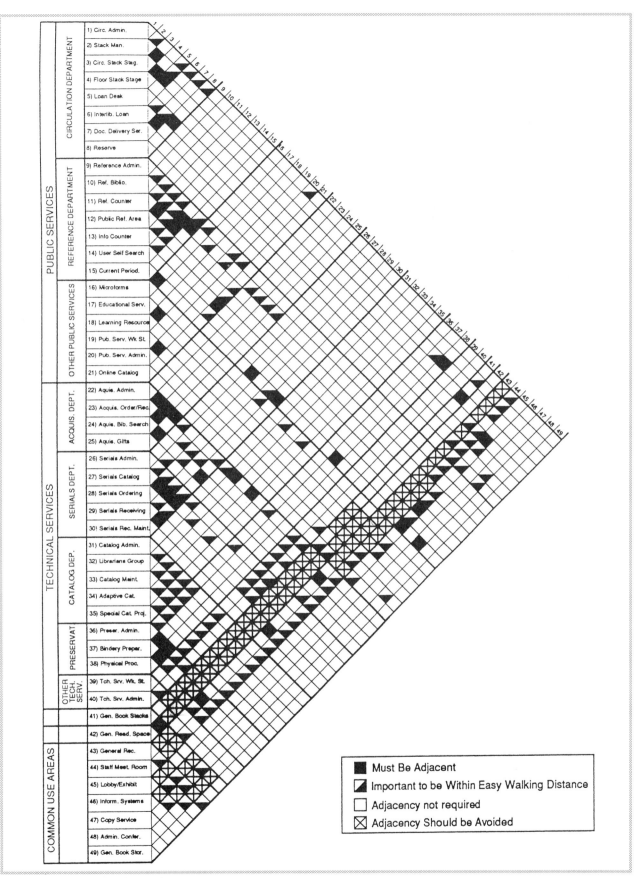

Figure 2. Functional Relationships Matrix

responses received from the library staff at UCI are represented by the matrix. The matrix shows those areas that must be adjacent, those that are important to be within easy walking distance, those for which adjacency is not required, and those for which adjacency should be avoided.[11]

Reading the matrix for area 41, the General Book Stacks area, the matrix indicates that adjacency must be avoided with working units 17 to 20 which include Educational Instruction and Public Services offices, and all areas from 22 to 40, or the entire Technical Services area. The General Book Stacks should be within easy walking distance of the Online Catalog and Dispersed Copy areas. General Book Stacks must be close to General Reader Space.

Although reading the matrix appears formidable for so many areas as are found at the University of California–Irvine, it does provide a quick reference to determining adjacency requirements.

Bubble diagrams are a simplistic but effective form of correlation diagram that tells the design professionals what functions and things need to be next to one another. Using circles, ovals and other simple geometric forms, bubble diagrams represent factors, functional elements or physical aspects, and lines between the bubbles indicate connection. They are an excellent decision-making tool which provides an opportunity for considering a variety of possible solutions to any given problem. They may be used for small, intricate areas within a building as well as for major areas.[12]

Bubble diagrams concentrate the design team's attention on function, since the sizes, shapes, and other physical requirements of objects are largely eliminated. Their key advantage is to provide a focus on how things might work in the most effective and efficient manner.

The shape of geometric figures used in bubble diagrams does not necessarily need to match the eventual shape of the space to be created. Usually the size of the geometric figures is of little consequence beyond the fact that larger circles or ovals usually indicate something that will require more space than a function or object represented by a smaller figure (fig. 3).

The juxtapositions of geometric forms express relationships, as follows:

1. Two figures that don't touch indicate two distinct and separate functions.
2. Figures touching indicate separate functions which must be next to each other.

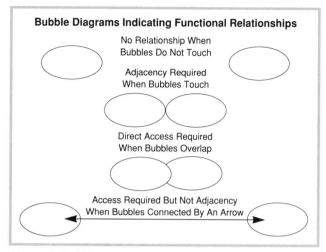

Figure 3. Bubble Diagram

3. Overlapping figures indicate functions which must be accessible one from the other.
4. Figures connected by arrows indicate access is required, but not necessarily immediate adjacency.

The best way to proceed with bubble diagrams is to start with a macro bubble representing major spaces and functions and move into more defined figures that represent smaller areas. Some of the information captured on bubble diagrams may be further refined by transferring it to analysis cards, which are described below.

Bubble diagrams have been programmed into computer graphic systems whereby the computer generates bubble diagrams automatically from relationship matrices to identify room relationship patterns and floor plan layouts.

Similar to, but more geometrically precise than a bubble diagram, a block diagram may be used to show the organization of functional or activity areas. Each area is represented by a square or rectangle that is proportionally sized to the relative amount of space

11. James Stirling and Michael Wilford, "University of California at Irvine Science Library: Detailed Project Program" (Irvine: IBI Group/L. Paul Zajfen, 1988).

12. Raymond H. Holt, "Using Functional Relationships (Bubble Diagrams) in Your Building Program," in *Planning Library Buildings: From Decision to Design*. Papers from a Library Administration and Management Association Buildings and Equipment Section Preconference at the 1984 American Library Association Annual Conference, Dallas, Texas, ed. Lester K. Smith (Chicago: American Library Association, 1986), 83–105.

required for the function. Arrangement of the blocks provides a preliminary layout plan for library committee approval and designer action (fig. 4).[13]

Analysis cards are a collection of index cards used to organize and reorganize programming information. Each card carries a single piece of programming data that contains either a short piece of text or a graphic description. A separate card is prepared for each programming element. A good format for the cards is a 5-by-8-inch index card because this format converts easily into 35mm slides for presentations. The example card illustrates some of the key accessibility factors that might come out of a brainstorming session by the design team when discussing a meeting room in a public library (fig. 5).[14]

The working advantage of the analysis cards is the ability to move a number of cards around on a flat surface to represent program elements and show relationships in the building space. In using analysis cards, some techniques to remember are:

1. Think the message through by reducing the information or idea to its simplest form. If the card is not big enough to hold all of an idea, odds are that the idea can be broken into smaller parts.
2. It is better to use visual images than words. If words are used, they should be labels no longer than one sentence. The objective is to get people to comprehend arrangements by glancing over the analysis card relationships.
3. Cards should be designed for display so that the designer can easily explain his or her concepts to the library building committee. Minimum letter height should be 1/8 inch, and pen-line width should be no. 2 or larger.

Link node diagrams are another relatively simple technique to show straightforward connections among elements in a program. The diagram consists of nodes that represent connected or unconnected elements and lines that link elements together. The size and position of nodes are insignificant. The connection of elements can be built up one-by-one and the resulting completed pattern will indicate clusters of related elements. Knowing what the clustering will be is a primary objective of simple link node diagrams. Sources of information about clustering are based on the rating or ranking of relationships between individual elements. The visual representation of clustering can be enhanced by illustrating the intensity of relationship between individual

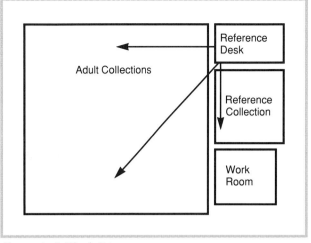

Figure 4. A Block Diagram

Figure 5. An Analysis Card

elements. This may be represented by line thickness or number of lines between nodes. The thicker the line or the more lines between connections, the more significant the relationship (fig. 6).[15]

In translating a library's program into schematic design, the library design team may use one or more of the above techniques.

Model Illustrating Conversion

One of the great mysteries of understanding design, by non-design-oriented people, is how to move from

---

13. Palmer, *The Architect's Guide to Facility Planning*, 130.
14. Ibid., 120–35.
15. Ibid., 128–29.

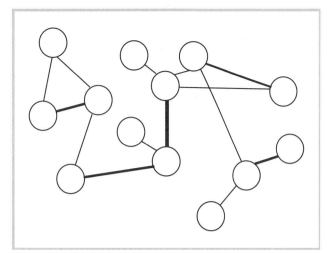

Figure 6. A Link Node Diagram

a completed building program into a design solution. Librarians understand and relate to building programs and programs are of great help in identifying function, defining it, justifying it, and quantifying it in terms of space needed. Librarians also are able to discern adjacencies between functions, such as loan of materials, collections, support services, work programs, etc.

The real mystery results because most librarians are not able to visualize the process because of the difficulty of translating data into two- or even three-dimensional space. Architects spend many years in formal education and training learning how to translate data into space.

In most cases, it is virtually impossible to demonstrate the creativity or the literally thousands of variables which must be dealt with by the architect in bridging that gap. The following case study is an attempt to do that.

The Case of Chula Vista

In this case study the process will be illustrated through a library program for a single-level library of approximately 35,000 square feet (gross) that is the regional library of the Chula Vista, California, Public Library. Design for the building is being developed by the San Diego architectural firm of Wheeler, Wimer, Blackman & Associates, and the building has been funded through a grant administered by the California State Library. This study reflects the firm's work, and demonstrates how library program and space

needs may be translated into physical form by using bubble diagrams and adjacency studies.[16]

The mission of the library is to service an established community with strong historical and traditional ties to its Mexican-American heritage. The regional library is located just a few miles from Mexico. The 1990 census and community studies indicate minimal growth in population occurring over the next twenty years. The service population is expected not to exceed 86,000 people.

The total assignable square footage is 27,944 sf with non-assignable spaces accounting for 7,000 sf. Total collections amount to 178,417 volumes and reader seats approach 500 spaces (see fig.7).

After identifying the basic program elements, the design team establishes the relationships of various elements in pictorial form. This is done through a series of bubble diagrams that help relate space to adjacencies. Through the constant adjustment of the bubbles, it is possible to observe the developing organization in space, and the importance of one space to another. The main areas of the library need to be shown with each individual bubble representing a library function, thereby showing relationships by the position of the bubbles.

It is important to refer to the building program constantly during this process. As options are considered, the design team will want to again test these alternatives against the program. External functions and their relationships must also be considered. At this point a simple question should be asked: Does it make sense? Options should be tested against basic building circulation and information transfer; and the staff should be asked if the relationships shown work for the library staff. Moving from the total area of the building, each area should be studied. In this example, macro bubble diagrams can be utilized for the public area and its adjacency to the circulation desk, lobby, and the children's library in order to study the relationships within the area. It is important to stay within the study loop until at least two good alternative solutions are determined. After at least two general solutions are developed, work should begin in smaller clusters like delivery or the children's area. Further refinement in both these areas can be achieved through the use of micro bubble diagrams.

---

16. Richard Blackman, "Library Planning from Program to Concept Design" (San Diego: Wheeler, Wimer, Blackman & Associates, 1991).

AREA	ASF	READER SEATS
Lobby	805	12
Browsing	1,841	26
Reference	3,197	54
Adult Services	5,962	62
Young Adult	831	16
Adult/Reference	760	
Children's Library	4,352	47
Story Hour		80
Workroom	590	
Technology User's Center	1,221	20
Circulation Desk	740	
Workroom	1,290	
Literacy Team Office	1,650	39
Study Rooms	400	16
Meeting Rooms	2,850	125
Administration	370	
Delivery	100	
Staff Lounge	430	
Custodial	205	
Storage	400	
TOTALS	27,994	497

Figure 7. Library Space Requirements

Groupings of bubble clusters along various building circulation patterns should now begin to be linked (see fig. 8). This will help to clarify lines of sight for control and supervision. Major and minor public and staff circulation paths should be tested for ease of information transfer. A plan to resolve the criteria should be tested against the program.

In this stage, do not overly complicate the organization of the clusters. In most situations simple, clear groupings will help to organize potential building shape. There is an obvious link between the circulation desk and the reference desk, and there is a core of spaces that revolve around the lobby and a core of spaces that revolve around the reference area.

Once the design team is satisfied that the first option works, the program should be tested against a second option (see fig. 9). Option two is depicted in a linear fashion. Note how lines of supervision are clearly defined between the circulation desk and reference desk, with browsing sandwiched between them. Note also how the lobby organizes public spaces, and maintains a link with the circulation desk. From the lobby it is possible to enter into the library proper past the circulation counter checkpoint, or, alternatively, go into other public spaces such as the meeting room or literacy center.

Obviously the purpose is to create lines of site and supervision. After the completion of the second option, the program should be revised. At this stage, the design team should solve problems of adjacencies, access, and square footage requirements. Refinement at this point may require rejecting or revising a program requirement. After all of these preliminary adjacency studies are completed, the site should be reviewed (fig. 10).

The key site issues to consider when locating the building are: vehicular and pedestrian access, view corridors, walking distance from parking lot to the building entry, transportation alternatives, pickup and drop-off zones, book drops, deliveries, trash, prevailing breezes, utilities, and solar orientation. Difficult sites require creative solutions. Site restrictions may require reconsidering the assumptions previously developed.

A simple graphic sketch identifying the basic elements of the site in a simple visual format clearly identifies possible constraints or opportunities available when locating the library on the site.

The site should be reviewed in relationship with the two alternative concept plans. From the option diagrams previously developed (figs. 8 and 9), things such as view corridors, prevailing breezes, northern light, entry points and delivery points should be considered for each option. Figure 11 shows the internal relationships as represented by the bubble areas against the site for option 1, and figure 12 shows the relationships for option 2.

The translation of the diagram is relatively simple, progressing to a suggested footprint for a building and a suggested site location. Both option 1 and option 2 should be reviewed again against this footprint.

North light, primary or secondary entrance points, and ease of deliveries and all other site elements must also be evaluated. The building footprint becomes a simple translation, by adapting the diagram and situating it on the site.

At this point the opportunities for internal planning focus on key elements. For example, the reference desk as a control point may be reviewed (fig. 13). The reference desk needs to be clearly identified to library users, and it should utilize those same lines of sight and supervision for adjacent space. A second example is the lobby and circulation desk (fig. 14). The circulation desk must be obvious to the incoming and exiting users. It should be close to browsing, it should have its own work space, and it should have suitable lines of sight to reference, the children's library, and public areas.

Building on a series of mini-solutions, the concept plan can easily be developed. Here's where the plan begins to articulate the true representation of space within the library. Concept Plan 1 (fig. 15) illustrates that the lobby is adjacent to the circulation

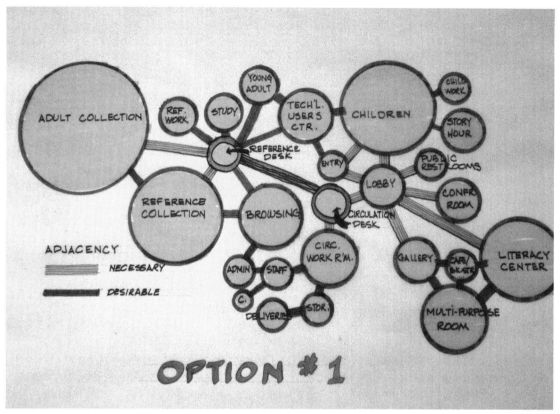

Figure 8. Linking Related Bubble Cluster Patterns

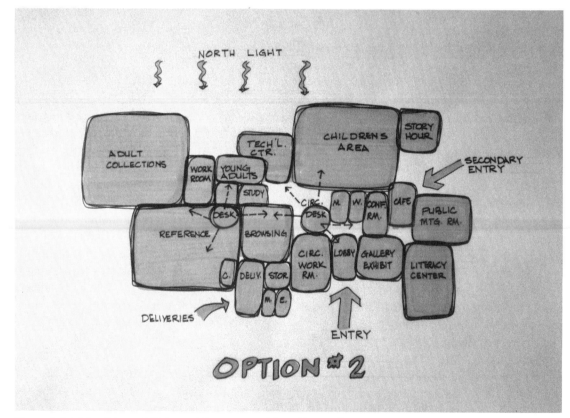

Figure 9. Linking Lines of Sight and Supervision Using Linear Patterns

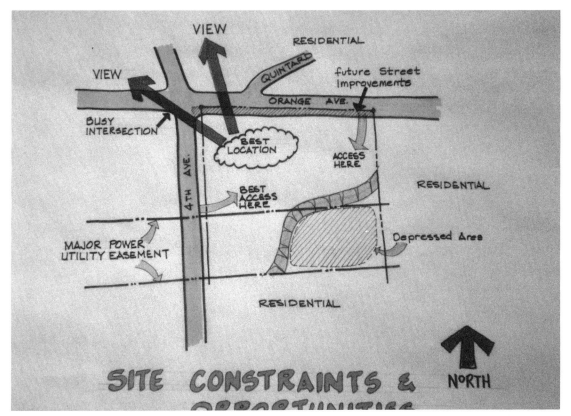

Figure 10. Site Review Sketch

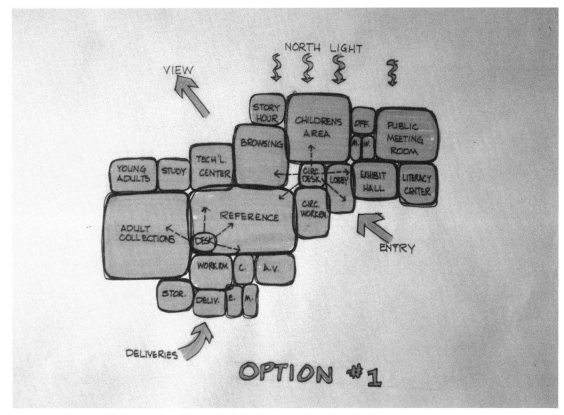

Figure 11. Internal Relationships Using Bubble Patterns (*see also* Fig. 8)

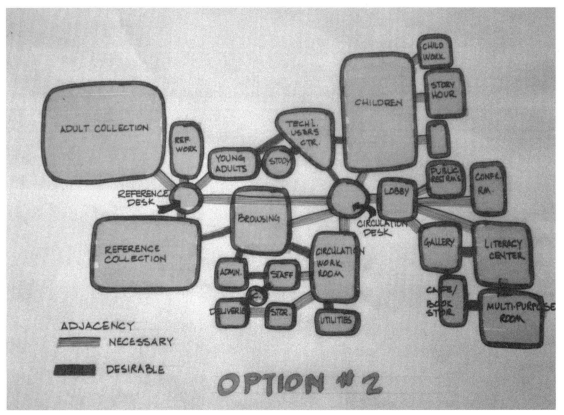

Figure 12. Internal Relationships Using Linear Patterns

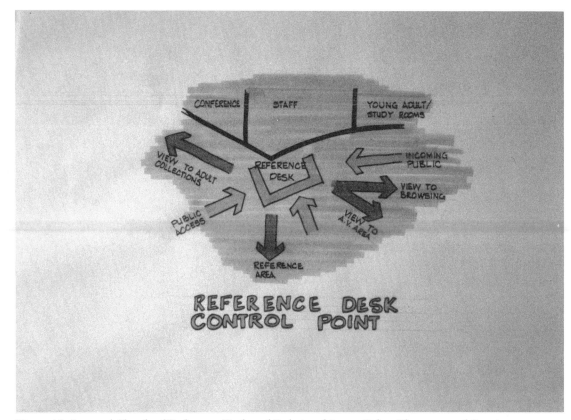

Figure 13. Internal Sketch of Reference Desk and Relationships to Other Elements and Services

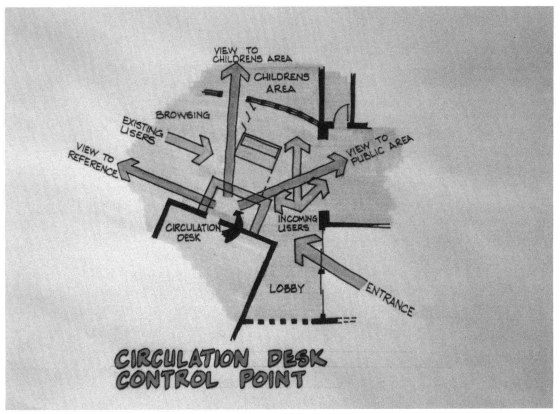

Figure 14. Internal Sketch of Circulation Desk and Relationships to Other Elements and Services

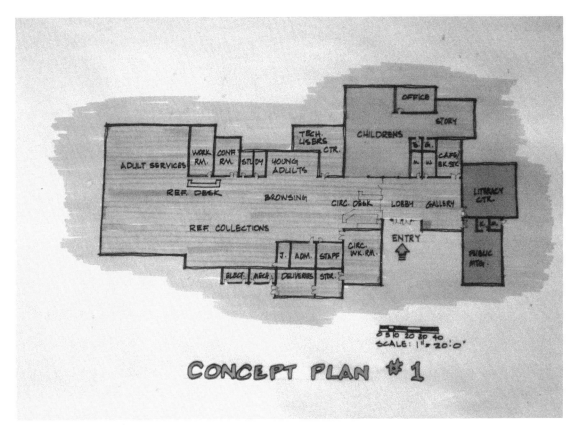

Figure 15. A Floor Plan Concept

desk, which has clear lines of sight to the children's library, to browsing, and to the reference desk. Reference, on the other hand, has successfully achieved observation of the collections, audiovisual, and browsing areas and the circulation desk.

When refining the concept plan, evaluate it again against the building program by asking these questions. Does it reflect the program's square footage requirement? Does it satisfy the program's essential needs? Does it relate to librarians? Follow the same suggested process in developing the second concept.

The second concept is selected by the design team, and the result is a formidable design which is classic in its approach, functional in its layout, aesthetically interesting, and offers multiple opportunities for design input.

To assist in the development of the refined plan, oftentimes, models are useful in articulating the massing of space as it relates to the comprehensive building design. Models give shape and establish an architectural character and, in general, they help to solidify the design.

By studying a model, the program may be further refined and adjusted to reflect the true identity and vision that was perceived when the process began. The final element in solidifying the translation from program to design is the creation of a rendered perspective.

Perspectives help to give scale, to give personality to the architecture and help articulate to the community how the library might appear in its final solution.

After all the work of taking the building program and translating program narrative into space needs is completed, seeing an architect produce a schematic design is a wonderful experience. But that experience only comes about after a lot of hard work, some compromises, and a whole lot of cooperation between the library team and the architect.

Selecting the Design Team

Donald G. Kelsey

During the early part of the building planning process that culminates in the writing of the building program statement, you have probably been involved with a team of people, mostly from within the library. Depending on how large and complex your library is and how complex the institution within which your library resides, your planning team was similarly complex. As you turn to the phase of the project where the building which will respond to the program needs you described in your building program will actually be built, an entirely new set of players is brought into the process.

For the purposes of this discussion, the term *design team* will be used to refer to that group of people the architect brings to the planning process. You will often hear the same term used to describe all of the parties who are involved in planning the building, including the library and other institutional participants in the process. The concept of a design team implies that we are not dealing with a single, individual architect, nor even a single architectural firm, but rather the staffs of many individual firms, each specializing in a particular aspect of the design process.

So what is the makeup of a typical design team? Usually, it includes the architect responsible for designing the project, a project manager, structural engineers, electrical designers and engineers, and the mechanical engineers responsible for designing and engineering the plumbing systems and the heating, air-conditioning, and ventilation systems. Often the interior designers are part of the architect's design team as well. More will be said later in this chapter about each of these roles in the design process.

For now, we shall focus on the selection process itself and your role as the library representative in that selection process. A number of people have likened the relationship between architect and librarian in a building project to a marriage. Sometimes, the selection process may look a lot like an "arranged marriage," where the librarian and the architect know virtually nothing about each other before they discover that they have been brought together to realize the design for a new building. At other times, it may seem that their relationship is the product of a long courtship, during which both parties were able to learn a great deal about each other. This kind of prior association will show how the design team is likely to approach the design task, as

Donald G. Kelsey is the director of Library Space and Preservation Planning at Meredith Wilson Library, University of Minnesota in Minneapolis.

73

well as reveal what the interpersonal styles of the other parties are like.

There is no "right way" to choose a design team. But it is important to recognize that there are certain characteristics of a selection process which, when properly understood, can enable you to develop your own strategy for being the most involved and credible player in that process as you can be.

What follows is a description of the way the selection process works in the academic world. The process in the public library world is described in the next chapter. However the basic steps in a typical design team selection are essentially the same for both. Let's begin with an overview of that process.

Steps in the Selection Process

It is typical for the design team selection process to take place after the building program statement has been written, the project has been approved by the governing or decision-making authority, and the planning funds for the project have been secured. The selection often takes place before the construction funds for the project are available. (An important part of the design process is determining the final construction budget.)

The typical steps in the selection process are:

1. Develop a list of architects
2. Send out a Request for Qualifications (RFQ)
3. Develop a list of most suitable firms[1]
4. Send out a Request for Proposals (RFP)
5. Review the proposals submitted
6. Develop a short list (usually not more than six firms)
7. Interview the firms
8. Follow up on interviews and proposals (checking references, site visits, additional interviews, etc.)
9. Make the final selection
10. Develop contract negotiations with selected firm

Develop a List of Prospective Firms

In many selection processes, a list of firms to be considered is developed. There are a number of sources from which such a list can be built. The American Institute of Architects (AIA) maintains lists of their membership. The ALA-AIA biennial library building design awards lists provide another source for the names of firms that have had experience

building libraries. It is important to remember that one or more successful library building projects in a firm's past does not automatically guarantee that the same firm will be as successful on your project. Similarly, a firm with no previous library design experience can turn out a very successful library design in its first attempt.

When developing your list, keep in mind that you need to investigate how your selection process works and what rules or regulations govern the process in your setting. State institutions in Minnesota, for example, are required to advertise requests for design services in a publication called the *State Register*. All of the firms in the state know about this method of solicitation, as do most of the architectural firms around the country.

Send out a Request for Qualifications

The process of requesting a separate statement of qualifications is not always necessary. It is often part of the Request for Proposal step. In fact, the whole focus of the design team selection process is mainly on the qualifications and experience of the proposers, *not* on the project itself.

Figure 1 is an illustration of a public notice for a library project. The first part is a generic statement of rules for acceptable proposals. You will see that they are quite stringent. Each time a design team is selected, at least one proposal is rejected solely on the grounds that the architectural firm did not follow the rules for submitting a proposal. This part of the process may seem excessively bureaucratic until one sits in on a selection review where there are no such rules and the volume of extraneous information included in many of the proposals is a real problem.

You will see that the information required speaks to the experience and qualifications of the proposer. There is only a brief description of the scope of the project itself.

Once a solicitation for design services is underway there will often be a rash of telephone calls and requested site visits from interested firms. You should identify very specifically who is going to answer

---

1. Steps 2 and 3 are not present in all selections. Sometimes the process moves directly to issuing a Request for Proposals. It is also important to remember that the major emphasis in the selection process is on the qualifications and experience of the firms making the proposals to take on this job and complete it successfully. The emphasis is usually *not* on the building program statement itself.

State Designer Selection Board

Request for Proposal for Two Projects

To Minnesota Registered Design Professionals

The State Designer Selection Board has been requested to select designers for two projects. Design firms who wish to be considered for these projects should deliver proposals on or before 4:00 p.m., September 18, 1990, to George Iwan, Executive Secretary, State Designer Selection Board, Room G-10, Administration Building, St. Paul, Minnesota 55155-1495.

The proposal must conform to the following:

1) Six copies of the proposal will be required.

2) All data must be on $8\frac{1}{2}$" $\times$ 11" sheets, soft bound.

3) The cover sheet of the proposal must be clearly labeled with the project number, as listed in number 7 below, together with the designer's firm name, address, telephone number and the name of the contact person.

4) *Mandatory Proposal contents in sequence:*

a) Identity of firm and an indication of its legal status, i.e. corporation, partnership, etc. If the response is from a joint venture, this information must be provided for firms comprising the joint venture.

b) Names of the persons who would be directly responsible for the major elements of the work, including consultants, together with brief descriptions of their qualifications. If desired, identify roles that such persons played in projects which are relevant to the project at hand.

c) A commitment to enter the work promptly, if selected, by engaging the consultants, and assigning the persons named 4b above along with adequate staff to meet the requirements of work.

d) A list of State and University of Minnesota current and past commissions under contract or awarded to the prime firm(s) submitting this proposal during the three (3) years immediately preceding the date of this request for proposal. The prime firms(s) shall **list and total** all fees associated with these projects whether or not the fees have been received or are anticipated. In addition, the prime firm(s) shall indicate the amount of fees listed which were paid directly to engineers or other specialty consultants employed on the projects listed pursuant to the above.

e) A section containing graphic material (photos, plans, drawings, etc.) as evidence of the firm's qualification for the work. The graphic material must be identified. It must be work in which the personnel listed in "c" have had significant participation and their roles must be clearly described. It must be noted if the personnel named were, at the time of the work, employed by other than their present firms.

The proposal shall consist of no more than twenty (20) faces. Proposals not conforming to the parameters set forth in this request will be disqualified and discarded without further examination.

5) *Statutory Proposal Requirements:*

In accordance with the provisions of *Minnesota Statutes, 1981 Supplement,* Section 363.073; for all contracts estimated to be in excess of $50,000.00, all responders having more than 20 full-time employees at any time during the previous 12 months must have an affirmative action plan approved by the Commissioner of Human Rights before a proposal may be accepted.

The proposal will not be accepted unless it includes one of the following:

a) A copy of your firm's current certificate of compliance issued by the Commissioner of Human Rights; or

b) A statement certifying that the firm has a current certificate of compliance issued by the Commissioner of Human Rights; or

c) A statement certifying that the firm has not had more than 20 full-time employees in Minnesota at any time during the previous 12 months; or

d) A statement certifying that the firm has an application pending for a certificate of compliance.

Continued

Figure 1. Example of a Request for Proposal

6) Design firms wishing to have their proposals returned after the Board's review must follow one of the following procedures:

a) Enclose a self-addressed stamped postal card with the proposals. Design firms will be notified when material is ready to be picked up. Design firms will have two (2) weeks to pick up their proposals, after which time the proposals will be discarded; or

b) Enclose a self-addressed stamped mailing envelope with the proposals. When the Board has completed its review, proposals will be returned using this envelope.

In accordance with existing statute, the Board will retain one copy of each proposal submitted.

Any questions concerning the Board's procedures or their schedule for the project herein described may be referred to George Iwan at (612) 296-4656.

7a) PROJECT—27-90
Walter Library Renovation
University of Minnesota

The University of Minnesota is planning to renovate the Walter Library building located on the Minneapolis campus. The existing building, completed in 1924, consists of 169,000 asf and 267,000 gsf. Walter Library has architectural importance for the campus because of the exceptional beauty and detail of the reading rooms and public spaces. It is one of the key buildings which were constructed to realize the design for the East Bank Mall designed by Cass Gilbert.

Typical of library buildings in the earlier part of the twentieth century, Walter Library has a stack tower designed with the book stacks as the structural element of the tower. The design makes very efficient use of the available storage volume, but has the possibility for catastrophic loss of life and collections in the event of a fire.

As the campus and library needs have changed, the existing facility no longer efficiently or safely meets the program demands. The existing facility must remain in use throughout the construction period. The architect must consider the on-going operations, phasing of work, schedule, and future operations in the design of the project. The construction budget is approximately $27,350,000.00.

Specific issues to be addressed in the renovation of the building include:
• General cleaning, patching, painting, and restoration;
• Fire protection;
• Air conditioning and humidity control;
• Improved electrical and telecommunications;
• Upgrade corridor wall fire ratings and provide two hour separation for the stack core;
• Provide the proper size and number of rated exits for all levels;
• Provide handicapped accessibility;
• Provide emergency and egress lighting;
• Evaluate the building shell to increase energy efficiency and reduce operating costs.

In addition, the renovation shall enable Walter Library to meet current library standards, maximize space utilization, and provide a high quality research and study facility. The organization of the facility must promote efficiency and ease of operation for both the users and the staff. It is necessary for the designer to prepare a long-term, flexible, and somewhat generic concept indicating how the building can best be utilized.

It is important that the overall design retain the historical aesthetic image of the building and preserve and enhance the site amenities. The designer shall have previously demonstrated restoration design ability and energy conscious design experience. Prior experience in the design of libraries is expected and experience with similar library restoration is desirable.

Figure 1. Example of a Request for Proposal (*continued*)

questions about the solicitation. Even so, you will usually receive requests from at least a half-dozen firms that want to come and look at the project in person. In such instances, make it a point to stress that they need to focus on their competence to take on the job, *not* on a preliminary analysis of how they will solve the design problem if they get the job.

Develop a List of Most Suitable Firms

The whole point of having a separate RFQ (Request for Qualifications) process is to make a first cut at identifying the firms that are most likely to be good candidates early in the process. This means planning a systematic review of each RFQ. Here, as at every step in the selection process, you need to find out how you can participate in the process. In some cases your participation will already be well defined; in other cases it will not be as obvious.

Send out the Request for Proposals (RFP)

This solicitation again has its major focus on the credentials of the firms; their previous related experience; their previous working experience with the electrical, mechanical, and other firms they plan to have in their design team; and their record in bringing projects to conclusion *on schedule* and *within the budget*.

The RFP may also ask for information about particular skills and abilities the successful proposer is expected to have. For renovation projects these may include experience with historic restoration and experience with renovating the heating and ventilation systems in old buildings.

Here again, the ground rules should be laid out clearly, describing what kinds of information *must* be included in a successful proposal and the submittal deadline.

Develop a Short List

When the deadline for proposals has arrived, the selection panel will want to meet as soon as possible to review the proposals and begin developing a short list of firms that will be invited to interview for the project. This should not exceed five or six firms, if at all possible.

Sometimes it is desirable to investigate references at this stage in the review process. Often the

selection onto the short list is made solely on the evaluation of the written proposals themselves.

Interview the Firms

Like all other steps in the process, the format for the interviews should be made clear in the invitation to the firms. The length of the interview should be clearly defined, including the limit you wish to set on the time the firm has to make its presentation. Typically the firm is allowed to make a presentation to the selection panel in whatever way it thinks best. This is usually followed with some discussion and questions from the selection panel. It is typical for a firm to make a visual presentation of its previous work, often with slides; so provision should be made to have a room with good audiovisual support. It is useful to schedule the interviews so that members of the selection panel may discuss each interview upon its completion. This helps the panel members to share impressions when they are fresh and raise questions that may need more follow-up before the final selection can be made.

Final Selection

In the final selection process references are thoroughly checked, if this has not happened earlier in the process. It is often advisable to arrange for the selection panel, or at least a portion of the panel, to make site visits to relevant examples of the firms' previous projects.

The site visits will be most useful if they can be coupled with ample opportunity to meet with the people from the staff who were responsible for planning the building, strategic staff who have responsibility for managing the building, as well as the maintenance staff, if possible. Note that some of the most useful post-occupancy evaluation information comes from the maintenance staff who spend their lives keeping the lights on, or fixing broken systems in the building.

If there is going to be a design competition, it often occurs at about this point in the process. All of the pre-selection steps that have led up to this point in the process are typical for choosing the few firms that will be invited to participate in a design competition.

Design competitions are very useful in a number of instances. Often all or part of the fund-raising for the construction of the building will rest on a campaign that will be greatly enhanced if there is already some idea of what the building will look like. There are other reasons for having a competition as well. Besides getting an idea of how the building's exterior might look, the competition can give the people who will be working with the design team a chance to see how prospective firms interact with their clients.

Design competition costs are usually the full responsibility of the competing firms. The costs are usually quite high because of the amount of work involved. Yet no matter how much money a firm spends on the competition, it does so knowing full well that it may not be awarded the job. Hence, the competition represents a substantial, and risky, front-end investment for any design firm to make. Sometimes the owner institution agrees to support the design competition with a modest stipend to the firms that compete, but this support is usually only a fraction of the actual cost of the competition.

A design competition also carries risks for the client. The usual focus of the competition is on the exterior of the building, with very little attention paid to the interior arrangement of functions and spaces. It is easy to fall into a kind of trap in which the institution becomes very taken with an exterior design, only to discover flaws in that design once the interior spaces begin to be developed.

I am aware of one competition in which the firms were asked to take the project almost all the way through schematic development. This involved substantial interaction with the client. There were perhaps three firms in this competition, which meant that the library had to be willing to essentially plan the building three times with three different design teams.

In some circumstances, an unsuccessful proposer may have developed a design element that you like. But asking the successful design team to incorporate that feature into their design raises several concerns of an ethical nature—concerns that may be very difficult to resolve.

Design competitions won't be an issue for most planners because they are not common, due to the expense for all parties involved. If a competition will be part of your selection process, I encourage you to give a lot of further study on how to plan the competition and to talk to others who have been part of the competition process before you just plunge into it.

Contract Negotiations

By whatever method, a design team is finally chosen for the project. At this point the institution will enter into a contract negotiation with the principal representative of the design team.

Architectural fees are usually budgeted into construction projects as a percentage of the total project construction budget. The actual setting of the fees and the specific contract language which lays out clearly what services the architect is expected to provide for a fee are matters for negotiation. For many years firms tended to work with established formula ranges set by the AIA. This is less common now.

With respect to services to be provided, will the design team be responsible for interior design and furniture selection, among other services? During the schematic and design development phases of the work, the contract often specifies how many sets of drawings the design team is expected to provide. Work beyond what is specifically outlined in the contract may be provided for either through amendments to the contract or by working out some sort of additional fees agreement that may be written into the contract.

Often the people who are actually involved in writing the contract are a different group of people than those who participated in the selection process. I encourage you to read the contract that is negotiated with your design team. There are a number of things that may be defined in the contract that you should know. Sometimes, for example, the number of meetings the design team is expected to attend may be defined. You need to know whether this is defined, otherwise you may find yourself incurring additional expenses that you were not prepared to meet.

The important thing to realize about contract negotiations is that the contract results in the design team's agreeing to provide an array of design services for a fixed fee. There are often some additional services provisions on a time-and-materials fee basis, but the great majority of the work is fairly well defined in the negotiation process and the fee is set. Requests for significant additional work beyond the understandings reached in the contract negotiation process will likely result in a request for additional compensation from the architect.

This understanding is important because it can have a significant impact on how smoothly the design process plays out.

Design Team Selection in an Academic Setting

The designer selection process in an academic institution is often highly organized and is often also largely the responsibility of persons outside the library. The authority for contract negotiations may rest only with the senior university administrator responsible for budget and finance. In another institution this authority may reside with the person in charge of the university planning office. Selection may require approval from the university's governing board, be that a board of regents, a board of trustees, or in the case of a private institution, the living relatives of founders of the college or university. In the event, the process is often complicated and difficult to understand.

A case in point is offered by a design team selection process I participated in at the University of Minnesota. There, we rely on the State of Minnesota's Designer Selection Board for all design team selections. This is an appointed five-member board that usually includes at least one architect, one engineer, and someone with a landscape architecture background. The board reports to the State Department of Administration.

The project involved the renovation of the seventy-year-old library on our campus. I am an ex-officio member of all library building committees and was intimately involved in the writing of the program statement. When the time came to advertise for the design team, I asked the university's project manager, an architect who is on our planning office staff, what role I might play in the selection process. He told me that, inasmuch as the selection process was the responsibility of the state Designer Selection Board, there was no role for me. I then asked him whether I could at least see the proposals when they came in. I also assured him that I would not slow down the process—a prime concern, since the time the university is given to read and comment on the proposals is quite short. In fact, I said that if for some reason I could not read the proposals promptly, I would waive that opportunity to do so.

I then asked whether I might submit comments on the proposals myself, on behalf of the library, to the Designer Selection Board. He thought this a good idea, and suggested that I be present when he and his colleagues reviewed the proposals in the planning office. That way, I could add my comments to theirs. I agreed that this would be the best way to

proceed, since I knew of several of the projects that were cited by various firms and would therefore be able to add to the discussion of the proposals in a number of ways.

A day or so later I called him to ask whether the Designer Selection Board interviews were open to observers. He said that they were. I then informed him that both the university librarian and I were interested in hearing the interview presentations. His response was to invite the rest of the members of the building committee to the presentations. (As it turned out, seven of the nine who were on the building committee attended the interviews.)

On the day of the interviews, I arrived a little early and, having already obtained the names of the members of the Designer Selection Board, I went around and introduced myself to each member of the board as he or she arrived. When I met the chairperson, he was especially happy to have me there and asked whether the university librarian and I would like to question of the presenters. I said that we would. He pointed out that there was not a lot of time for questions, and I assured him that we would probably not ask each presenter more than one or two questions.

At the close of the interviews, the Designer Selection Board convenes and makes their selection immediately. I was astonished when the chairperson walked over to invite the university librarian and me to stay for their discussion, and for the balloting as well. It turned out that as the field of candidates was being narrowed there was one firm still in the running with which I had had a *very* bad previous experience. I asked for the privilege of making some additional comments before the final balloting and I believe that because I was able to offer some fairly concrete evidence of difficulty in working with that particular firm, we affected the final vote positively and that firm was not chosen.

The point to be made here is, if I had accepted the first answer I received about participation in our designer selection process, I would have spent the whole time sitting back in my office with no input into the process.

The Design Team

You should see clearly in a good proposal how the firms submitting the proposals plan to organize their design team. As mentioned earlier, nowadays design proposals are rarely submitted solely from a single architectural firm. Much more common is a proposal that may link two architectural firms and bring in structural engineering, mechanical engineering, electrical engineering, and interior design expertise from separate firms that are working as subcontractors to the firm responsible for the project.

There are a number of critical players who should be clearly defined. One individual will be designated the principal architect for the design team. This individual is essentially the final authority for answering design questions. There may be several architects working on the project over the course of its life, but the principal architect is expected to sort out the differences of opinion and present a unified design concept.

Only slightly less important in the overall success of the project is the project manager. This individual will be on the staff of the firm that is providing the principal architect. This person is an expert in the mechanics of bringing projects to a successful conclusion. Developing and refining the project budget, setting the project schedule, arranging meetings, and putting together all of the relevant information for each step of the process are typical tasks for this relatively new group of design professionals. This person is usually the main contact between the client and the design team.

The skills of the project manager are critical to bringing the design work along in a timely way. In fact, the reputation of an architectural firm can be greatly enhanced by having capable project managers on its staff who can bring complicated projects to completion on time and within budget. Quite frequently, this person is also the manager from the design team responsible for making sure that construction is proceeding according to the established schedules.

Often the electrical, telecommunication, and mechanical design services are provided by designers and engineers who come from entirely separate specialty firms, which are all working under the direction of the principal architect's firm as subcontractors in the design process. It is the responsibility of the principal architect—or more likely the project manager—to orchestrate the work of all of these firms throughout the design process.

The names of the firms that will provide the various engineering services required for the project *and* the names of the individuals from those firms who will be assigned to the project should be spelled out in the design team's proposal.

The design team actually includes a number of individuals from the library and its parent institution as well. The library will be represented by either the library director or someone designated to be the principal library representative. If the individual who represents the library through the design process is not the library director, that individual should have close communication with the library director and the authority to speak for the library in planning meetings. It is altogether likely that library directors who intend to be the principal representative in this process for their library will enjoy the task a lot more if they plan the rest of their administrative life as though they were going on leave for the duration of the project.

The institution will have one or more representatives on the design team as well. In the university setting this is a staff architect who is assigned by the university planning office to be the university's project manager for the duration of the project. At the University of Minnesota, once the point of construction is reached, the role of the project manager decreases somewhat and a person who specializes in construction management is assigned to see the project through the construction phase.

Often the institution's building code enforcement office will be represented on the design team, as will those people with responsibility for specific concerns such as life safety, handicapped accessibility, etc. In private institutions it is also common for the governing board to have a representative on the design team.

How library consultants get involved varies as well. There are several common patterns of library consultant involvement. In some instances, the library retains a consultant to help develop the building program statement. That individual may or may not be a sitting member of the design team. The library may choose to continue using a consultant for advice on critical design decisions as the project moves through its development. The library may ask the consultant to make periodic reviews of the plans at various stages of completion and make comments to the library director.

In some settings, the library consultant is retained either by the library or by the architectural firm with principal responsibility for the project. The consultant is a sitting member of the design team. The consultant may not be expected to be present at all meetings of the design team, but is a significant player in the design team makeup. As such, he or she is sometimes called on to resolve differences during the design process.

A third configuration is one in which the consultant is retained by the architectural firm to serve as an expert advisor. This situation is much like the first one in that the consultant is not a formal member of the design team, but is available to the architect and the design team as needed to help the architect develop design solutions and to critique proposed solutions before they are presented to the design team as a whole.

The Architectural and Interior Design Phase

The design team has been put together; you have identified the people who will be involved in a significant way from the library; and you have decided who will represent the other key interests from your institution. Now, at last, it's time for the actual design process to get underway!

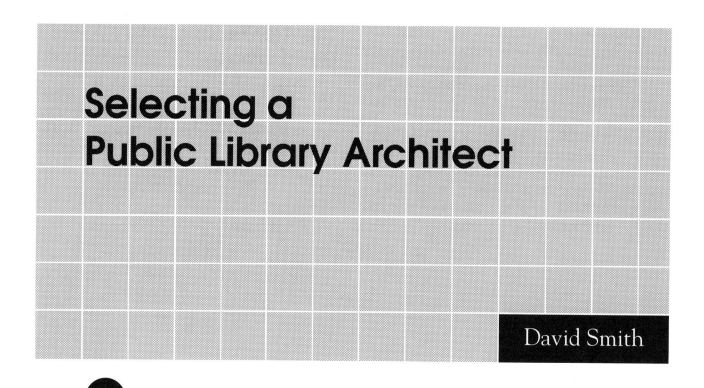

Selecting a Public Library Architect

David Smith

Selecting the right architect is an important decision that will have a major impact on the successful outcome of the project. In selecting the best-qualified project team, look for the proper balance of:

Communication skills
Aesthetic/design skills
Technical expertise
Cost estimation
Common sense

Don't just select a "firm." Consider the work experience and interview those individuals who will actually be actively involved in your project.

The vast majority of architects know less about public libraries than you do. Their judgment may be further flawed by romantic recollections of the ivy-covered library of their childhoods. Communicate, listen, and educate, but be assertive and lead the situation.

A library building planning project that is dominated by the library board or library architect without major participation of the library staff and input of users will generally result in a poorly planned, inadequate library.

David Smith is a consulting librarian in Hopkins, Minnesota.

The normal point of selection comes after approval has been granted and planning funds allocated. The architect can be selected before the written library building program is completed so long as basic information on the project is provided that indicates the size of the project and scope of the work.

The process outlined may also be used to select a professional interior designer. Many architectural firms do not have interior designers on their staffs and it will be necessary for the architect or the library to find someone who possesses these necessary design skills.

Basic Steps

1. Develop a list of prospective architectural firms
   Local sources
   Other libraries
   State library
   State chapter – American Institute of Architects
   Architects requesting consideration
2. Extend Request for Qualifications or Request for Proposals
   Describe scope of work and information desired
   Request uniform information

3. Preliminary Selection

Evaluation of responses to Request for Qualifications or Request for Proposals

Library building committee – Representatives from city or county library

Prepare "short list" for interviews – Six firms maximum

4, Interviews

Oral, visual presentation by the architects in the firm who will be working with library

Rating by library building committee or library board

5. References/Inspection of Work

Inspection trip to selected candidates' completed buildings

Reference check of selected candidates

6. Final Selection

May require supplementary information or second interview

7. Architect Contract

Full – May include more specific language than the standard American Institute of Architects form

Additional services – Interior design, furniture selection

Process and Criteria Utilized in Selecting a Public Library Architect

As already stated, the selection of an architect is one of the most important decisions a library board and director will make in the course of a building project. The firm will be given responsibility for designing and supervising the construction of the most functional and aesthetically pleasing building possible with the budgeted funds. There are many architectural firms of varying size and competence that would welcome the opportunity to participate in the building project. Thus, with a substantial number of firms from which to choose, it is important that the selection be based on established objective criteria, as well as on the selectors' subjective and intuitive interpretation of the supporting information presented by the architects in writing and at the interviews.

The fee involved should not have a substantial bearing on the selection since most firms will follow a fairly standard rate based on the American Institute of Architects' suggested fees. Fees will normally run between 8 percent and 10 percent of the total construction costs—which include the general construction contract costs and electrical and mechanical installation. Expansion or renovation fees will run 1 percent to 2 percent more, due to the complexity and need for greater technical analysis. The conditions of employment and resulting fees must be thoroughly discussed. Offers to work for extremely low fees must be examined carefully. If there are no special contract arrangements with the architect for assistance in furniture selection and other work in building interiors, some additional payment may be necessary. This payment may be arranged on an hourly basis, not to exceed a certain limit. Any special conditions relating to the project must be discussed thoroughly with the architect in conjunction with the fees proposed.

Frequently the architectural firms being considered are requested to provide a proposal based on a process that divides the project into two phases. Phase 1 is the initial work required to develop site plans, schematic designs, estimates of cost and, if necessary, a model to use as information and supporting materials to secure the necessary funding for the project. Phase 2 includes completion of design preparation of working drawings and specifications. It should be recognized that there is a fair amount of time put into these early planning documents since they will set the design and funding foundations for the entire project. The architect must have sufficient information from schematic design to develop cost estimates that are accurate. It is both time-consuming and embarrassing when insufficient attention is paid to these concerns and the project supporters have to return to the community for additional funds once the actual planning begins in earnest. Most architects calculate that this phase of the project requires time and expense equalling approximately 15 percent of their total fee. Frequently, this is done on an hourly basis with a "not-to-exceed" figure. A firm that offers to assemble this information at little or no cost may not address the initial planning needs as fully as it should, but will expect to recover the full fee during Phase 2. Information on how the firm approaches and costs out the initial phase may be solicited in the request for qualifications and discussed during the interviews.

The project will require the services of an individual with excellent interior design skills or appropriate consultants since both the functional layout of the building and the furnishings and general aesthetics are of primary importance.

If an interior designer is also employed, it is desirable to involve this individual early in the planning phase so that functional design and layout of the library complements general building requirements. Any necessary adjustment between function and form of the building must be made in the design stage. Many architectural firms do not have a level of interior design skill and knowledge of shelving and furniture that an experienced interior designer brings to the project. An interior designer may be selected to work as a consultant to the library on this project, or an architectural firm may obtain these design services subject to approval of the library.

News of this public library building project in area construction and other publications may result in a substantial number of applications. Under normal conditions, the selection process may be completed in three months.

The first major step in the selection process involves the information that is gathered in the Request for Qualifications (RFQ) or Request for Proposals (RFP), extended to firms applying for consideration in the selection process. The RFQ asks for more detailed and specific information on proposed methodology and fees. The purpose of the forms used is to gather relevant information regarding a firm's background, capabilities, and previous projects so that the library building committee may review the submissions and evaluate the firms on a comparable basis to determine which firms will be invited to interview.

The second step, preliminary selection, reduces the number of applicants to be interviewed to five or six firms. It is desirable to include an experienced city building official and representative from the city council in the selection process. Information in terms of background, general capabilities, and experience in library projects is reviewed by the library building committee to determine if the architect is well qualified to do the library project and should be interviewed. (See the evaluation sheet, fig. 1.)

Once the preliminary selection stage is completed, arrangements may be made for formal interviews. It is desirable to set the interviews for one or, at most, two successive days so all presentations will receive equal recall on the part of the library building committee. Each firm should be given a fixed amount of time, normally an hour, for its presentation and related questions and discussion. In fairness to all, the scheduling is followed as closely as possible, with breaks for discussion between each interview. It is anticipated that the architect will bring audiovisual material to the interviews and will be invited to do so.

The library building committee gathers the same information from each firm based on questions which have been prepared in advance. If additional questions are raised during the course of the interview and the answers are important, the firms interviewed before the questions arose will be given an opportunity to submit a short written response, An interview rating sheet based on questions and responses is useful.

During the course of the interview, the architect is not expected to provide specific solutions to the project; rather, the library building committee determines through general questioning the overall qualifications of the architect for this project. In addition to elaborating on requested information, the discussion with the architect should cover to the committee's satisfaction the following questions:

1. Who in the firm will be responsible for the library project from beginning to end and how will this individual approach the job? It is important to interview persons with whom the library will be working, not an official of the firm who turns the work over to the back office upon his or her return.

2. What is the architect's current work load? Will the library be given immediate and complete attention? What does the architect view as a realistic schedule in which to complete basic elements?

3. What is the architect's method of communication when dealing with others? Is the architect someone with whom the library staff will feel comfortable and work well? Since developing an acceptable building design requires a good deal of give and take, excellent communication skills must not be overlooked.

4. How well does the architect appear to know his or her field? What are the strengths of the firm in design, project management, engineering, and other special areas of expertise? In the case of a small firm, what other resources will the firm utilize in developing its plan?

5. What has been the architect's experience in establishing and maintaining budgets on recent projects? What is the firm's recent experience with construction costs and project bidding?

6. What specific or related experience has the proposed project architect had that qualifies him or her to design a library?

ARCHITECT EVALUATION SHEET

David R. Smith, Consulting Librarian

Evaluated by: _____

Date: _____

FIRM NAME _____ PROPOSAL RANKING ____ INTERVIEW RANKING ____

Name(s), position(s) of
persons interviewed.

Rating Scale
5 - Superior
3 - Satisfactory
0 - Unacceptable

Library Building or Comparable Design
Experience of Team Members

Historic Building/Expansion
or Other Unique Skills Required

Experience of Team Members

Interior Design/Skills Experience
of Team Members

Project Team–Organization
Project Experience

Line of Communication
and Responsibility

Understanding of Project
Objectives and Scope

Communication

     Written–

     Responses to RFP?
     Questions–

     Verbal–

Cost Estimation and Control

Ability to Manage a Project of this Nature

Strengths of Project Team

Weaknesses of Project Team

Overall Evaluation

    Rating Scale
    5 - Superior
    3 - Satisfactory
    0 - Unacceptable

Consider for Interview?

____ Yes

____ No

____ Maybe

GENERAL COMMENTS:

Figure 1. Architect Evaluation Form

7. What has been the architect's approach to designing buildings of similar size and type? Do you like this architect's design work?

8. From the architect's point of view, what conditions do handicapped access codes and energy codes impose on this type of project?

9. What is the architect's approach to interior design to achieve the most efficient functioning of a building? Does the firm utilize an interior designer? Information on services in the area should be provided.

10. How is the architect's fee schedule determined? How does the nature of the project affect the fee? If selected, what would the architect charge to develop the necessary schematic and elevation drawings, construction estimates, and a model to satisfy Phase 1 design and secure the necessary funding? What has been the firm's experience with similarly phased projects?

After the library building committee has reviewed all of the requested information provided by the architect and interviewed those firms in which it is interested, it is desirable to visit at least one completed building of the firms under final consideration, if this has not already been done. References must be gathered from previous clients. Once this point is reached and all the information reviewed, the final decision may still involve some reliance on the subjective view of the library building committee regarding which firm being considered would work best with the library staff and other participants on the project to create a most functional and attractive public library.

Symbols and Specifications

Charles Smith

Architectural drawings and symbols are widespread within our society. Most of us have used the floor diagrams in shopping malls, when looking for an apartment or a house, and in our own library handouts. These diagrams provide only location and general size of areas. Construction drawings show a great deal more information. It takes a lot of hard, sometimes difficult, work to prepare a set of documents for the bidding process.

After several meetings with the architects, you will begin to see some schematics. Schematics are used to determine relationship of areas and their approximate sizes. You will also begin to see more information added to the drawings as the schematics develop through the preliminary drawings and the final working drawings. There is a need for recording decisions that are made in consultation with the architect. The architects' tools for recording this information are in drawings and verbally in what are called specifications. Learning to read these documents need not be difficult. There are numerous books on reading drawings (sometimes called blueprints) and on specifications. With some effort on your part, drawings will begin to make sense. Specifi-

Charles Smith is a research development librarian at Sterling C. Evans Library, Texas A & M University in College Station.

cations, although verbal, also require some getting used to as they have a language of their own. Both the final working drawings and the specifications make up part of the package known as the contract documents.

The Contract Documents

The construction contract documents consist of several parts. Each part has a particular purpose and appears in some form in almost all major building projects. Although this chapter focuses on symbols used on the drawings and on specifications, it is important for one to see now they fit into the whole of the documentation. The construction contract documents consist of the following:

Invitation to Bid

The invitation to bid means that whoever receives a copy is invited to bid on performing the work of constructing the building according to the contract documents. While the list of firms receiving the invitation to bid can be controlled, it is important to remember that the bidding process is based on competition. It is usually beneficial to allow more bidders. For public work, the law will generally require that the invitation be published in a prescribed form in a newspaper.

Instructions to Bidders

These instructions tell each bidder how to prepare the bid in order to ensure that all received bids will be in the same format and can be more easily compared.

Bid Forms

Bid forms are used to provide a uniform arrangement for ease in fair and equitable comparisons of the bids.

Bond Forms

A bond is a legal document that binds someone into the contract, thereby assuring that the contractor will perform as agreed.

Form of Agreement

The form of agreement is sometimes thought of as the contract; however, it is only a part of the complete package. The agreement identifies the parties of the contract, the work to be performed, a statement of costs, the time elements involved in the construction of the building, and the signatures of all parties concerned.

General Conditions of the Contract for Construction

The general conditions define the contractual relationships and the procedures relative to the project. The AIA Document A201 is used most often to fulfill this part of the documentation.

Supplementary Conditions

The supplementary conditions are used to modify the general conditions where they do not meet the requirements of the particular project being bid.

Addenda (if issued)

Addenda are used to modify proposed contractual material during bidding.

Drawings

The drawings are used to visually identify the materials upon which the contract is based, and to define their physical relationship.

Specifications

The specifications are used to define the quality and types of workmanship and materials upon which the contract is based.

The Construction Drawings

A set of construction drawings will contain several subsets named to reflect the intent of their contents. Each drawing is identified with an alphanumeric page number indicating the subset and page sequence; e.g., "S32" will identify the 32nd sheet within the structural drawings.

Architectural Drawings

The architectural drawings contain the measured floor plans, the exterior and interior elevations, sections, and enlarged details. Sometimes the site plan, demolition plan, and landscape plan are also included in the architectural drawings rather than in a separate set.

Structural Drawings

Structural drawings detail how the frame of the building is to be put together. They show the framing plan of each floor with details of all critical junctions.

Electrical Drawings

The electrical drawings show all electrical work connected with the project. These are the drawings that locate all outlets for electricity, telephones, and computers if conduits are used.

Mechanical Drawings

Heating, ventilating, and air-conditioning (HVAC) locations and requirements are shown on the mechanical drawings. Included will be the location and sizes of duct work and the location of HVAC machinery throughout the building.

Furniture Layouts

The location of all furniture and stacks are shown on the furniture layouts.

Specialty Drawings

There are times when some items are not included on other drawings. Some specialty drawings might be for the building graphics, separate landscaping, or elevators.

Architectural Symbols

Often, schematics begin to take shape as line drawings during consultation between the librarian and the architect. Working closely with the architect during this phase will prepare you for the symbols found in the later drawings. You will find that architects will explain the drawings to you, indicating the meaning of all lines and symbols. Learning does not need to happen all at once. As you discuss the needs of your library with the architect, you will see sketches of ideas being developed. After a short time, most people begin to recognize walls, doors, and windows and to some extent the materials being discussed. Before long a line starts to mean a wall of a particular construction. You begin to recognize a break in the line as the door, for example. Make sure that you obtain full sets of drawings for your review at several stages of their progress. Allow yourself plenty of time to study the drawings.

The complete set of drawings will use many symbols to convey a great deal of information in relatively little space. Usually a legend will appear on the first sheet on each subset of drawings. Each subset of drawings will therefore have its own set of symbols. Somewhere on each sheet of drawings can be found the scale used for that sheet. A common scale used is 1/8 inch equals one foot—written as $1/8'' = 1'$. Often several drawings will appear on the same sheet, each with its own scale indicated.

Some typical symbols used on the architecture portion of the drawings are shown in figure 1. Parallel lines drawn to scale will be filled with different symbols to indicate the type of wall intended, e.g., a fill of dots with randomly placed small irregular circles indicates a structural concrete wall. An arrow overlaid with a circle will indicate where a section is cut, while the numbers inside of the circle indicate the drawing number and the sheet on which that section is drawn. There are many books which list these and additional symbols used on drawings. It will soon become apparent that in order to discuss details with the architect at least a simple vocabulary of these symbols is necessary.

It is not unusual for one to take a "walk" through the drawings and "see" if the spaces are what is expected. As you view the drawings, try to visualize all aspects of an area in order to determine whether it will function well. Check for such items as sufficient electrical and computer outlets, and lighting fixtures in the needed areas. Now is when you need to make sure that the drawings reflect the needs of the library. Make necessary changes before the contract is bid. Did the architect meet the stated needs as presented in the building program? Do the drawings reflect what was agreed upon during your discussions?

With increasing frequency, drawings are produced with the aid of computers. Many, if not most, architects have found that computers make easier work of the base layouts and the various required overlaying for added information. Base drawings with added room names and dimensions can be sent on a floppy disk to the structural, electrical, and mechanical engineers for their work on the project.

Preliminary furniture layouts can begin to take shape and will help the electrical and mechanical engineers properly locate outlets for utilities and other special requirements. Various information for a particular area of the building will be reflected on different drawings. You can overlay pairs of drawings and then hold them up to a bright window. This technique will aid you in finding misplaced items. One common pair of drawings is the utilities outlets sheet, located in the electrical set, with the furniture layout as the overlay. It will thus become more readily apparent to you when, for example, telephones and electrical wires are inconveniently located or sited in places where they'll only get in the way.

By the time the preliminary drawings are approved, work may already have begun on the final

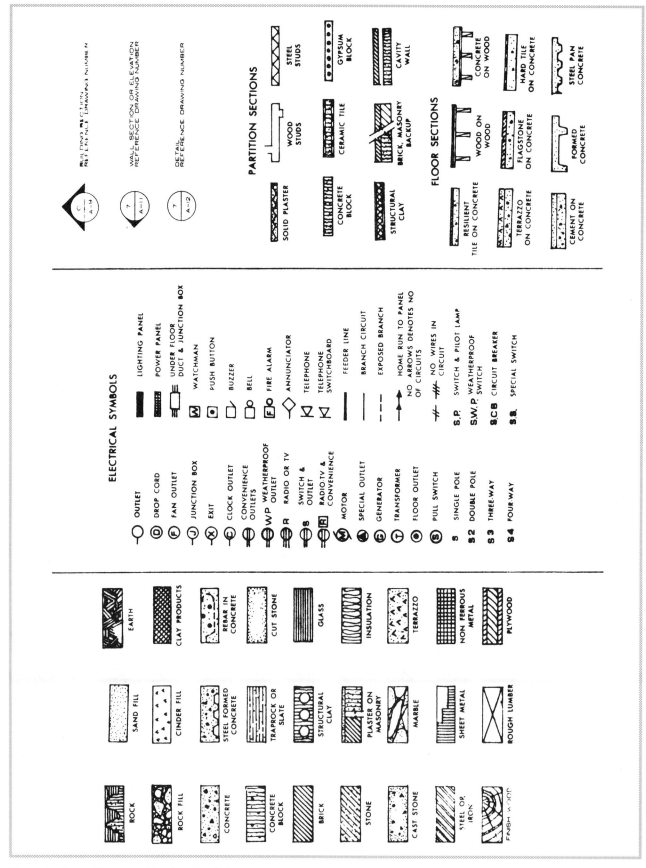

Figure 1. Some Common Graphic Symbols

drawings. These final drawings (or working drawings, as they are also called) are the ones which will become part of the contract documents. It is a must that you stay familiar with the progress of the drawings and with the other parts of the contract documents. Some areas may require modification as the drawings enter their final stages.

Specifications

The specifications should be developed along with the drawings and should, therefore, offer no surprises. You may need to ask for a set of specifications before the bidding process; try to get them as early in the project as possible. Some architects may want to delay the writing of specifications until most of the design decisions have been made. With the use of computers in the design office, early specification outlines are easier to produce and should evolve along with the drawings.

The information shown on the drawings and indicated in specifications complement one another. Care is required in order that the two do not contradict each other. The *Construction Specification Institute's Manual of Practice* states: "Specifications define the qualitative requirements of products, materials and workmanship upon which the contract for construction is based. The full intent and content of the Contract for Construction cannot be fully expressed by words or drawings, each acting independently of each other. Specifications and Drawings are complementary and for that reason must be created as parts of equivalent value to the whole."[1]

Specifications follow a particular order which has been agreed upon and is the same in most cases.

Technical Specification Divisions

Division 1 – General Requirements
Division 2 – Sitework
Division 3 – Concrete
Division 4 – Masonry
Division 5 – Metals
Division 6 – Wood and Plastics
Division 7 – Thermal and Moisture Protection

Division 8 – Doors and Windows
Division 9 – Finishes
Division 10 – Specialties
Division 11 – Equipment
Division 12 – Furnishings
Division 13 – Special Construction
Division 14 – Conveying Systems
Division 15 – Mechanical
Division 16 – Electrical

Each of the above divisions is in somewhat the order in which the work will be done. The divisions are also further broken down into subdivisions like those shown in the following example:

Division 6 – Wood and Plastics
06050   Fasteners and Adhesives
06100   Rough Carpentry
06130   Heavy Timber Construction
06150   Wood–Metal Systems
06170   Prefabricated Structural Wood
06200   Finish Carpentry
06300   Wood Treatment
06400   Architectural Woodwork
06500   Prefabricated Structural Plastics
06600   Plastic Fabrications

One can see that there is room for growth within this division, much like a library classification scheme. It can also be noted that not all areas will apply to every project. The writer of specifications will delete the inappropriate areas and may, on occasion, add an area for a particular project. Figure 2 is a page from a set of specifications. Note that related specifications are cross-referenced and that the tone of the text is direct. "Shall be" is a frequent phrase, as is "or approved equal." Following the heading on products-materials there is a section outlining fabrication requirements and how the installation is to be carried out.

This brief introduction will not make you into experts. You should, however, find that it has provided you with a beginning skill from which to work.

---

1. Construction Specifications Institute, *CSI Manual of Practice*, rev. ed. (Alexandria, Va.: Construction Specifications Institute, 1985), I-1-2.

Section 06200

FINISH CARPENTRY

(See General Provisions, Supplemental General
Provisions, and Special Provisions as they apply)

PART 1 - GENERAL

1.1   DESCRIPTION

A.   Scope: This work comprises finish carpentry, millwork and casework.

B.   Related Work Specified Elsewhere:
1.   Marble counter tops in Section 04450.
2.   Wood doors in Section 08200.
3.   Plastic laminate faced doors in Section 08250.

1.2   QUALITY ASSURANCE

A.   Material Grading: The grades of lumber and plywood used shall be as defined in
the latest edition of AWI Quality Standards, Sections 100 and 200, and as
defined by the rules of the recognized associations of lumber and plywood manufacturers producing the materials specified.

1.3   SUBMITTALS

A.   Shop Drawings: Submit shop drawings of millwork and casework to the Architect
for review before any work is fabricated.

1.4   PRODUCT DELIVERY

A.   Deliver millwork and casework to the job site only when dry and protected storage space is available at or in the building so that it can be kept dry and
protected from injury.

1.5   JOB CONDITIONS

A.   Protection: Erect and maintain protective covers over finish wood sills and
jambs of openings being used for traffic and the handling of materials.
Millwork damaged through neglect of the above requirements shall be repaired or
replaced without additional cost to the Owner.

PART 2 - PRODUCTS

2.1   MATERIALS

A.   Interior Wood: Lumber shall be kiln-dried to a moisture content between
6% and 11%.
1.   Pine: For woodwork, casework and millwork.
a. Lumber: AWI Premium grade white pine or southern pine selected to produce a first class paint finish.
b. Plywood; AWI Economy-grade natural birch or medium density resin fiber
surfaced plywood (US Plywood Cabinet Grade) selected to produce a first class
paint finish.

06200 - 1   1450

Figure 2. Sample Specifications

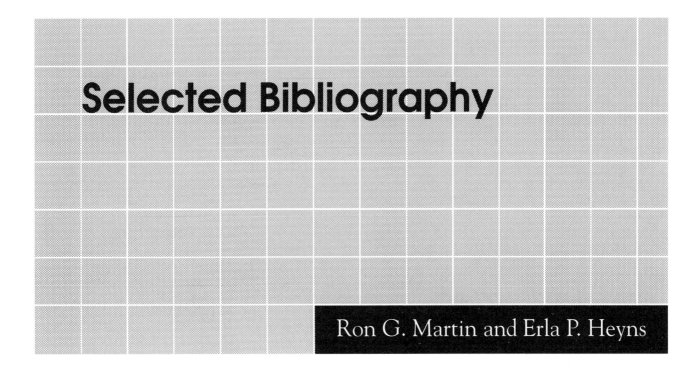

Selected Bibliography

Ron G. Martin and Erla P. Heyns

American Institute of Architects. *Architect's Handbook of Professional Practice*. Washington, D.C.: American Institute of Architects, 1963–Annual.

Americans with Disabilities Act (ADA) Accessibility Guidelines for Buildings and Facilities: Proposed Rule, Architectural and Transportation Barriers Compliance Board. 36 CFR Part 1191 (Docket No. 90-2) RIN 3014-AA09. Published in *Federal Register*, January 22, 1991. 56 (14); 2323-2395.

An Architect's Guide to Building Codes and Standards. 2nd ed. Washington, D.C.: American Institute of Architects, 1990.

Bareither, Harlan and Jerry L. Schillinger. *University Space Planning: Translating the Education Program of a University into Physical Facility Requirements*. Urbana: University of Illinois Pr., 1968.

Beckman, Margaret. "Cost Avoidance in Library Building Planning: What, Where, When, Why, Who?" *College Library Journal* 47 (1990): 405–9.

Blackman, Richard. "Library Planning from Program to Concept Design." San Diego: Wheeler, Wimer, Blackman & Associates, 1991.

Boss, Richard W. *Information Technologies and Space Planning for Libraries and Information Centers*. Boston: G. K. Hall, 1988.

Brown, Carol R. *Selecting Library Furniture—A Guide for Librarians, Designers, and Architects*. Phoenix, Ariz.: Oryx Pr., 1989.

Brown, Walter C. *Blueprint Reading for Construction: Resi-dential and Commercial*. South Holland, Ill.: Good-heart-Willcox, 1990.

Brownrigg, Edwin B. "Library Automation: Building and Equipment Consolidations in Implementing Computer Technology." In *Advances in Library Administration and Organization*, no. 1. Greenwich, Conn.: JAI Pr., 1982. 43–53.

Cohen, Aaron and Elaine Cohen. *Designing and Space Planning for Libraries: A Behavioral Guide*. New York: R.R. Bowker, 1979.

Construction Specifications Institute. *CSI Manual of Practice*. rev. ed. Alexandria, Va.: Construction Specifications Institute, 1985.

Cooper, Michael D. "A Cost Comparison of Alternating Book Storage Strategies." *Library Quarterly* 59 (1989) 239–60.

Crawford, Walt. *Current Technologies in the Library—an Informational Overview*. Boston: G.K. Hall, 1988.

Creative Planning of Special Library Facilities. Ed. Ellis Mount. New York: Haworth Pr., 1988.

Dahlgren, Anders. *Planning the Small Public Library Building*. Small Libraries Publications, no. 11. Chicago: American Library Association, 1985.

_____. *Public Library Space Needs: A Planning Outline*. Madison, Wis.: Wisconsin Department of Public Instruction, 1988.

_____, ed. *Library Trends*. Urbana, Ill.: University of Illinois Graduate School of Library and Information Science, 1987.

_____. *Wisconsin Library Building Project Handbook.* 2nd ed., Madison, Wis.: Wisconsin Department of Public Instruction, 1990.

Davis, Robert J. "Mira Mesa Library Design Development." San Diego: BSHA, 1991.

Downing, Jeff and June Koelker. "Infomart: Intelligent Design, Intelligent User." *Library Hi Tech* 5 (1987): 77–99.

Drabenstott, Jon. "The Consultants' and Vendors' Corner: Designing Library Facilities for a High Tech Future." *Library Hi Tech* 5 (1987): 103–11.

Ellsworth, Ralph E. "ABC's of Remodeling/Enlarging an Academic Library Building: A Personal Statement." *Journal of Academic Librarianship* 7 (1982): 333–43.

_____. *Academic Library Buildings.* Boulder, Colo.: Associated University Press, 1973.

Energy Conservation in New Building Design (ASHRAE Standard 90, rev. 1980) and *ASHRAE Handbook* (annual). Atlanta: American Society of Heating, Refrigeration and Air Conditioning Engineers, Inc.

Feilden, Bernard M. Between Two Earthquakes: Cultural Property in Seismic Zones. Marina del Rey, Calif.: Getty Conservation Institute, 1987.

Finney, Lance C. "The Library Building Program: Key to Success." *Public Libraries,* (1984): 79–82.

Galvin, Hoyt R., ed. *Planning a Library Building: The Major Steps.* Proceedings of the Institute Sponsored by the American Library Association Buildings Committee at St. Paul, Minnesota, June 19–20, 1954. Chicago: American Library Association, 1955. p. 3-18.

Gordon, Wally. "Gaming Techniques Used in Developing Schematic Design." San Diego: Deems, Lewis, McKinley, 1991.

Healey, Edward H. "Planning a Library in One Week." *American Libraries* 22 (1991): 302–4.

Hoke, John Ray Jr., ed. Ramsey/Sleeper Architectural Graphic Standards. 8th ed. New York: Wiley, 1988.

Holt, Raymond M. *Planning Library Buildings and Facilities —From Concept to Completion.* Metuchen, N.J.: Scarecrow Press, Inc., 1989.

_____. "Using Functional Relationships (Bubble Diagrams) in Your Building Program." In *Planning Library Buildings: From Decision to Design.* Papers from a Library Administration and Management Association Building and Equipment Section Preconference at the 1984 American Library Association Annual Conference, Dallas, Texas. Lester K. Smith, ed. Chicago: American Library Association, 1984. 83–105.

Hudson, Kathy. "Historic Buildings and Modern Technology: The California State Library Remodels for Automation—A Case Study." *Library Hi Tech* 5 (1987): 49–58.

IES Lighting Handbooks. vol. 1, *Applications,* and vol. 2, *References.* New York: Illuminating Engineering Society of North America, 1984.

"Information Technology and Space Planning." *Library Systems Newsletter* 5 (1985): 81–83.

Johnson, Jane G. (ed). *Library Buildings Consultant List.* Chicago: Buildings & Equipment Section, Library Administration & Management Association, American Library Association, 1989.

Kaser, David. "Academic Library Buildings: Their Evolution and Prospects." In *Advances in Library Administration and Organization,* no. 7. Greenwich, Conn.: JAI Pr., 1988. 149–60.

_____. "Current Issues in Building Planning." *College & Research Libraries* 50 (1989): 297–304.

_____. "Twenty-five Years of Academic Library Building Planning." *College & Research Libraries* 45 (1984): 268–81.

Kusack, James M. *Post Occupancy Evaluation Manual: Guidelines for Evaluating Library Buildings.* New Haven, Conn.: The Author, 1989.

Leighton, Philip D. and David C. Weber. *Planning Academic and Research Library Buildings.* 2nd ed. Chicago: American Library Association, 1986.

Library Administration and Management 1 (1987): 76-106. (Library Buildings issue)

"Library Buildings." Ed. Anders C. Dahlgren. *Library Trends* 36 (1987). (Library Buildings issue)

"Libraries from Inside Out." *American Libraries* 20 (1989): 297–351.

"Library Furniture." *American Libraries* 19 (1988): 261–307.

Library Journal. 112 (1987): 45–76. (Library Building issue)

Lieberfeld, Lawrence. "The Curious Case of the Library Building." *College & Research Libraries* 44 (1983): 277–82.

Liebing, Ralph W. *Architectural Working Drawings.* 3d ed. New York: Wiley, 1990.

Life Safety Code (NFPA 101) and Life Safety Code Handbook. Quincy, Mass.: National Fire Protection Association, 1991.

Lushington, Nolan and Willis N. Mills, Jr. AIA, *Libraries Designed for Users, A Planning Handbook.* Syracuse, N.Y.: Gaylord, 1979. 60–110.

McAdams, Nancy R. "Trends in Academic Library Facilities," *Library Trends* 36 (1987): 287–98.

McClure, Charles R., et al. *Planning and Role Setting for Public Libraries: A Manual of Options and Procedures.* Chicago: American Library Association, 1987.

Marti, Manual Jr. *Space Operational Analysis: A Systematic Approach to Spatial Analysis and Programming.* Mesa, Ariz.: PDA Publishers, 1981.

Mason, Ellsworth. "Writing a Building Program." *Library Journal* 91 (1966): 5838–5844.

_____. *Mason on Library Buildings.* Metuchen, N.J.: Scarecrow Press, Inc., 1980.

Meier, Hans W. *Construction Specifications Handbook.* 4th ed. Englewood Cliffs, N.J.: Prentice Hall, 1989.

Michael, David Leroy. "Technology's Impact on Library Interior Planning." *Library Hi Tech* 5 (1987): 59–63.

Morris, John. *Managing the Library Fire Risk.* 2nd ed. Berkeley, Calif.: University of California Office of Risk Management and Safety, 1979.

Muller, Edward J. *Reading Architectural Working Drawings.* 2nd ed. Englewood Cliffs, N.J.: Prentice-Hall, 1981.

Myller, Rolf. *The Design of the Small Public Library.* New York: R.R. Bowker, 1966. Out of print but available at state libraries.

National Fire Protection Association. *Life Safety Code Handbook.* 4th ed. Quincy, Mass.: National Fire Protection Association, 1988.

_____. *NFPA 232AM, Archives and Record Centers.* Quincy, Mass.: National Fire Protection Association, 1991.

_____. *NFPA 910, Protection of Libraries and Library Collections.* Quincy, Mass.: National Fire Protection Association, 1985.

National Library Service for the Blind and Physically Handicapped. *Planning Barrier Free Libraries, A Guide for Renovation and Construction of Libraries Serving Blind and Physically Handicapped Readers.* Washington, D.C.: Library of Congress, 1981. (Note: Subsequent legislation may have affected these guidelines.)

National Research Council, Committee on Preservation of Historical Records. *Preservation of Historical Records.* Washington, D.C.: National Academy Press, 1986.

Novak, Gloria. "Building Planning in Austerity." *Austerity Management in Academic Libraries.* John F. Harvey and Peter Spyers-Duran, eds. Metuchen, N.J.: Scarecrow Press, 1984: 185–204.

_____ ed. "The Forgiving Building: A Library Building Consultants' Symposium on the Design, Construction, and Remodeling of Libraries to Support a High-Tech Future." *Library Hi Tech* 5 (1987): 77–99.

Ontario Ministry of Citizenship and Culture. *Building Libraries: Guidelines for the Planning and Design of Public Libraries.* Toronto: Queen's Printer for Ontario, 1986.

Ontario Ministry of Culture and Communications. *Assessing Your Community for Library Planning.* Toronto: Queen's Printer for Ontario, 1986.

Palmer, Mickey A. *The Architect's Guide to Facility Planning.* Washington, D.C.: American Institution of Architects, 1981.

Peterson, Kenneth G. "New Storage Facility at Southern Illinois University." *College & Research Libraries News* 51 (1990): 39–43.

Planning Library Buildings: From Decision to Design. Papers from a Library Administration and Management Association Buildings and Equipment Section Pre-conference at the 1984 American Library Association Annual Conference, Dallas, Texas. Lester K. Smith, ed. Chicago: American Library Association, 1986.

Poage, Waller S. *Plans, Specs and Contracts for Building Professionals.* Kingston, Mass.: R.S. Means, 1987.

Ramsey, Charles George. *Ramsey/Sleeper Architectural Graphic Standards.* 8th ed. John R. Hoke, ed. New York: Wiley, 1988.

Rawles, Beverly A. and Wessels, Michael B. *Working with Library Consultants.* Hamden, Conn.: Shoe String Press, 1984.

Rickert, Suzan. *Campaigning for Libraries.* Wheat Ridge, Colo.: Central Colorado Library System, 1988.

Robinette, Gary O. *Barrier-free Exterior Design: Anyone Can Go Anywhere.* New York: Van Nostrand Reinhold, 1985.

Rosen, Harold J. and Tom Heineman. *Construction Specifications Writing: Principles and Procedures.* New York: Wiley, 1990.

Rush, Richard D., ed. *The Building Systems Integration Handbook.* New York: Wiley, 1986. (especially Chapter 6, Integration for Performance)

Sannwald, William W. *ALA/LAMA/BES Architecture for Public Libraries Committee. Checklist of Library Building Design Considerations.* 2nd ed., Chicago: American Library Association, 1988.

Scott, Wendy. *The Accessible Canadian Library: A Planning Workbook for a Barrier-free Environment.* Ottawa: National Library of Canada, 1986.

Sommer, Robert, "Reading Areas in College Libraries." *Library Quarterly* 38 (1968): 249–60.

Stirling, James and Michael Wilford. *University of California at Irvine Science Library: Detailed Project Program.* Irvine: IBI Group/L. Paul Zajfen, 1988.

Styles, Keith. *Working Drawings Handbook.* 2nd ed. London: Architectural Press, 1986.

Uniform Building Code. Whittier, Calif.: International Conference of Building Officials, 1991 (latest edition).

Uniform Federal Accessibility Standards (FED-STD-795, revised 1988). Issued jointly by the U.S. General Services Administration, Department of Defense, Department of Housing and Urban Development, and the U.S. Postal Service.

United States Architectural & Transportation Barriers Compliance Board. "Proposed Americans with Disabilities Act (ADA) Accessibility Guidelines for Buildings and Facilities." *Federal Register,* January 22, 1991; 56 (14) 2323-2395.

Wakita, Osamu A. *Professional Practice of Architectural Working Drawings.* New York: Wiley, 1984.

Werking, Richard Hume, "Collection Growth and Expenditures in Academic Libraries: A Preliminary Inquiry." *College & Research Libraries,* 52 (1991): 5–23.

Young, Virginia, ed. *The Library Trustee: A Practical Guidebook.* 4th ed. Chicago: American Library Association, 1988.

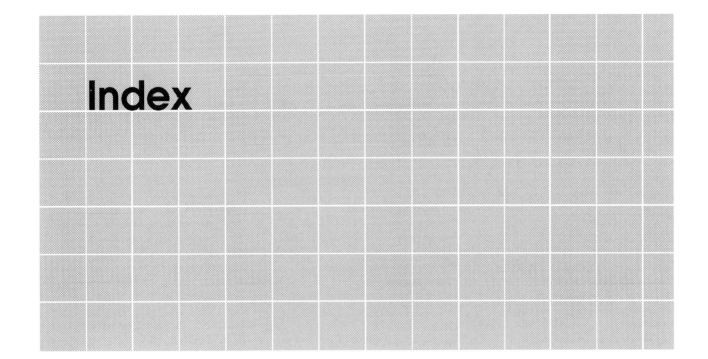

Index

Ron G. Martin has served for the last twelve years as associate dean for public services at Indiana State University Libraries. He holds two master's degrees, in library and information science from the University of Missouri and in educational media from Indiana State University. Among his most recent publications are two articles in *Library Hi Tech* on the design, development, and evaluation of an online catalog workstation. Martin has directed the writing of a library building program statement for an academic library and maintains an avid interest in the future design and development of library buildings.